Dear Bob,

merry X mas

may the peace of

be with you.

Remembering always what

we shared.

Your Brother +

Son in Jesus

Joe Marinic

Two Dancers in the Desert

The last photograph of Charles de Foucauld,
taken in front of his house in 1916.

Charles Lepetit

TWO DANCERS IN THE DESERT

The Life of Charles de Foucauld

Foreword by
CARLO CARRETTO

ORBIS BOOKS
Maryknoll, New York 10545

Translated by John Griffiths from the French, *Plus loin sur la piste . . . Charles de Foucauld,* copyright © Les Editions du Cerf, Paris, 1981. This translation copyright © 1983 Search Press Ltd.

First published in Great Britain 1983 by Burns & Oates Ltd., Wellwood, North Farm Road, Tunbridge Wells, Kent, TN2 3DR, in association with Veritas Publications, 7/8 Lower Abbey Street, Dublin, and Dove Communications, 60–64 Railway Road, Blackburn, Victoria 3130, Australia

U.S. edition published by Orbis Books, Maryknoll, NY 10545

Orbis hardcover, 1983, ISBN 0-88344-511-5

Foreword
by Carlo Carretto

It is not difficult to introduce a book as enjoyable as this one, which deals with a person as fascinating as Charles de Foucauld.

This is an original book. The author has done what he set out to do. He has written from the depths of his heart and engaged the reader in an open and honest dialogue.

The book, then, is original; I should like to explain exactly what I mean by this.

Many people who have been gripped by the life and character of Charles de Foucauld have written about him. Their books seem to set a person before us adequately. They characterize, pigeon-hole and portray the individual competently. This book is different. Its author unequivocally declares that he is trying to present the identity of someone who, in the end, essentially, is inexplicable. Some people will find this approach rather odd, although of course the author has done his best to let available records speak for him whenever they are appropriate. As I see it, he wants his biography to help us to get really close to his subject. He wants to help us search directly for enlightenment, even if doing so often means entering that real darkness in which we have to live our life on this earth – with all its painful decisions, apparent contradictions and uncertain steps forward.

The central image which the author uses to grasp the essential mystery of Charles de Foucauld, is that of an invisible dance of two main characters on the road of life. They are man and God, two partners who are always in search of one another.

This idea alone is surely enough to make the book significant, and to offer the reader something quite new. It may seem unfortunate, then, that the author has been so reluctant to work out the implications of the image, and has left it to the reader to discern the major intervals of silence between one movement of the dance and another. Was he afraid, perhaps, that his idea might seem a trifle banal?

Far from it. He has found the genuine glowing pearl of mystical enlightenment and held it out to us so that we can look into its depths and see the true measure of human sanctity. That is probably the real value of a book like this, and what will make it interesting above all to young people who know nothing about the mystic of the Sahara but are looking desperately for someone who can help them on their harsh way through the wilderness of life.

Though none of us is wholly aware of it, each of us is looking for his or her life's partner – to escape loneliness, anxiety or sadness, or all three; and each of us often feels like a new and awkward dancer who is not quite sure as yet of his or her own self.

Charles de Foucauld was precisely that kind of dancer – a bit out of place because he was so out of the ordinary. God was his obvious and wholly attentive partner, helping him to take the right steps and guiding him so that he stayed on life's strange dance-floor; teaching him to aim for the ultimate reaches of love; looking ahead and secretly intervening to obviate any really bad slip-ups or absolute disasters.

What an amazing partnership! In the end it was the very same relationship that we all have with God, but one that was especially meaningful for someone like Charles de Foucauld; for someone who was always liable to wheel about suddenly, and therefore needed the unfailingly sensitive response of his divine partner if he was to keep his balance.

De Foucauld was an aristocrat and yet he had to learn to humble himself infinitely. He was a man of action who had to discover how to be still. He was impetuous and intense, and had to learn the meaning of caution and patience. He was a thorough-going colonialist, yet he made a major contribution to the liberation of the enslaved and to the struggle for the rights of the oppressed. He was patriotic and proud of French might, yet he had to make his own a love which transcended frontiers in order to realise his idea of fraternity. He could not abide any form of dirt or vermin, yet he lived among nomads who had no water to wash with. He had engraved the name Jesus on his heart, and had to force himself not to pronounce that name in the presence of those who preferred to hear of Muhammad.

Charles de Foucauld was by no means a born dancer, yet his

partner succeeded in leading him into a way of life so extraordinary as to convince us that we have been shown the limit-
less power of sanctity and the efficacy of grace in the face of all
human weakness.

Openly, intelligently, this biography tells of the difficulties
and contradictions among which Charles de Foucauld lived
and which he had to reconcile.

After reading these pages everyone, I am sure, will feel that if
God can so basically change the heart of such an individualist,
there is no limit to what he can do with us – who are no less
subject to difficulties, and experience no fewer ups-and-downs.

Strange, but it is so. In the past the fashion was for immobile,
unalterable saints who were incapable of any kind of sin, and
who followed an unswerving course to paradise. Today we are
more concerned with saints who, like us, stumble, make mistakes and live among contradictions but yet give us some reason
to hope. Charles de Foucauld helps us to hope. If someone like
him, living in improbable circumstances among the Touareg in
the heart of the Sahara, and unable to bring a single one of the
people there to accept the Christian faith, wrote: 'I am ready to
go to the ends of the earth for the Gospel's sake', he gives us
some reason to hope. If a man of action such as he, full of
practical ideas and with many human contacts, says to us:
'Today the entire village is celebrating and no one will come to
see me. My God, what joy to spend eight hours in prayer before
you, incessantly to petition and to love you', he teaches us to
hope. If an intellectual like Charles de Foucauld, a quite
exceptional linguist for his day, summarized his rôle as a
missionary among the indifferent in this one sentence: 'I shall
proclaim the Gospel with my life', he helps us to understand
where in the future hope is to be found, hope for us and for the
Church.

Finally, I should like to make one more point: Charles de
Foucauld followed the same route as Francis of Assisi. Like
Francis he underwent a radical conversion. He was poor and,
like Francis, he wanted neither works nor building but witness.
Like Francis, he lived in an age replete with problems for the
Church and for the world.

I have often wondered about the reason for this natural,
almost necessary similarity between the Saharan mystic and
the saint from Assisi. Now the answer seems simple: both of
them lived in an age which suffered from the same social and

religious contradictions but also the same pressure for an authentic return to the Gospel. Both Francis of Assisi and Charles de Foucauld found an answer to the demands of the age in devoting all their power and strength to trying to live the Gospel and love Jesus of Nazareth. Because they were both extraordinarily human, they succeeded in condensing the complexities of their search and the contradictions of their times into two incisive ideas: the notion of poverty and that of universal love.

Here is the secret of both men – what makes both of them so attractive to everyone and can fundamentally change anyone fortunate enough to get close to them.

They were poor; they believed in poverty; they lived as the poor live. But more than that, they knew how to love. They practised a love which knew no boundaries and was offered to all people without distinction of race, culture or religion.

Contents

Introduction

I imagine myself in the street questioning passers-by.

'Charles de Foucauld? . . . Don't know anything about him.'

'Charles de Foucauld? . . . He changed my life.'

'Charles de Foucauld? . . . I think a lot of him but I find him rather discouraging. I'm not a hero, you see.'

Three years ago, if someone had stopped me in the street and questioned me like that, I should have replied like the second passer-by: 'He changed my life'.

Since then, however, I have found out something. It took me aback at first. I even found it shocking. But now I find it a source of happiness.

This discovery did not fall out of the sky onto the pavement. It took three years of tough research work before it happened. My thanks are due to the many authors who have collected together so much material for me to draw on.

Now I am sure of my discovery. And I am in a position to reassure my third passer-by: even someone who is not a hero can have unusual things happen to him or her.

Charles de Foucauld, you see, is not a hero. He was a man of flesh and blood like you and me. He was complex and difficult to sum up. He had his ups and downs. He looked about him, went off the beaten track, got annoyed, was surprised, did stupid things, like anyone else. His story is like that of any lover.

I want to tell you that story in a very straightforward way. I shall do it with a number of flash-backs, individual scenes that often do not follow a strict chronological order.

In a way this is not a biography. It is more of a portrait, or rather a lightning sketch.

When you begin to read it you may say that all the details I give make it sound rather like a novel, and wonder if it is really historically accurate. I can assure you that each detail has been checked. In a few, minor instances some of the details are imagined, but these are well within the bounds of probability.

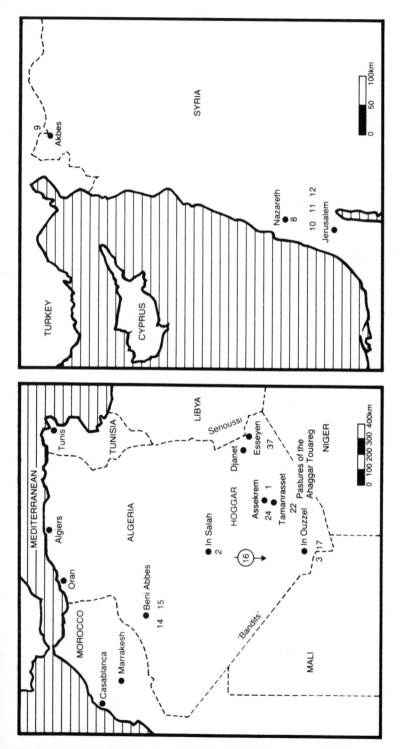

The figures on the maps indicate the relevant chapters in this book.

I

The wounded man on a camel

8 May 1902. In the Hoggar mountains at the centre of the Sahara. It was still night. A goat began to bleat.

Under the goat-skin tent nearby the women were at their usual household work. One child was still sleeping, but not a single man.

The mothers and a few slaves were trying to relight the fire of the day before and preparing to milk the goats. Everything was done in silence, in a way which suggests that people have not yet quite woken up. Their long dark-blue tunics reached to the ground. Large black veils were draped around them.

The new fire of a May day began to disclose their faces and projected fantastic shadows on the tent walls. The wonderful smell of thornbush smoke filled the air like incense.

They had to hurry. Otherwise they would not be in time to gather the grass they needed for the goats.

The beasts were bleating strongly now. The child woke up and rose to drink the fresh milk.

But where were the men?

The feeling of insecurity which had gripped the encampment for a few weeks once again affected the child. During the last few evening hours his mother had told him stories of famous battles from which the Touareg always emerged victorious. But in the daytime they spoke only of the column of Infidels (as the Muslims called the French) who were scouring the area, armed to the teeth.

They were in fact 135 Arabs under the command of a French officer.

The French had just completed their conquest of the northern Sahara. Now they had decided on a punitive expedition. The pretext for it was quite out of proportion to the size of the party sent.

A mad seven-week-long pursuit had led them to the heart of the Sahara, into the Hoggar, the land of the Touareg. An enemy had never before come so close. Already here and there they had burned homes and harvest. They had gone so far as to commit sacrilege by destroying the mosque of a neighbouring small village.

The Touareg assembled from everywhere around. The news went from camp to camp, like wild fire. That was why there were no men in our encampment. Sure of victory they had all gone in pursuit of the enemy party.

The child emerged from the tent. He was wearing a kind of long shirt.

The air was rather cold even though it was May. The valley was still damp after the heavy storm of the day before.

The sun was still hidden behind the mountains. But a whole section of the great range which surrounded the little valley was beginning to turn purple. In the north the high peaks (2000m–3000m, or 6500 ft–9500 ft) were already glinting. At their feet craters of the most extraordinary shapes simulated a moonscape.

Suddenly the women's cries caught the child's attention. Two camels were approaching slowly. On one of them a wounded Touareg was tied down with ropes which stopped him from falling off. The women of the camp moved forward unhurriedly.

The incredible had happened. For the first time ever the Kel Ahaggar had been put to flight. It had happened the day before, one day's journey away. The fight had lasted two and a half hours. Almost a hundred members of the tribe had given their lives in defence of their land.

The daring and the guns of the Infidels had vanquished the courage, numbers, spears and guns of the Kel Ahaggar. An apocalyptic storm had separated the two sides.

For the child a world had collapsed. The longing for revenge would never leave him.

The day of the Infidels[1]

At Amassara[2] *both sides were pushed to the limit,*
What with spears and the rifles of the infidels
And the unsheathed taheleh *swords.*
I ran upon the enemy, I struck and was struck
Till I was covered with blood all over as with a coverlet,
Pouring all over my shoulders and arms.
The girls who make music will not hear it said
 of me that I hide among the rocks.
Is it not true that thrice I fell, and thrice I was picked up,
And that, unconscious, they tied me with cords
 on the back of a camel?
And, because of that,
Defeat was no dishonour.
The infidels of old were victorious over the Prophet himself.

1 Poem written by the Touareg who was being carried on his camel.
2 Name of the valley which was fought over, near Tit.

2

The victory of the vanquished

19 January 1904. Near the In Salah oasis.

The caravan of twenty-four Touareg elders moved forward at camel's pace. It had covered over four hundred miles on its way northwards after leaving the Hoggar. It was only a few miles from the oasis of In Salah, where there was an infidel garrison. Peace had to be made with the French.

Make peace? Not everyone agreed. But Musa thought this was the best course.

Musa, the son of Amastane, riding his finest camel, was at the head of the caravan. Born into poverty, and orphaned at an early age, he had to remain satisfied with looking after his uncle's camels. Then things changed. At sword-point he had won a chieftain's reputation from one end of the Sahara to the other.

How could this warrior of nearly forty years of age make peace with the French?

The reason was to be found at the southern limits of the Sahara, a short way over the Mali frontier. There Musa had known for some years a *marabout*, or man of God, named Baï. Ten years had passed since their first meeting.

Baï appeared with his face veiled, one thin hand wrapped in cloth and telling his beads of amber and coral. He was short and unpretentious and was often silent, but when he spoke his slow discourse was full of wisdom. He spoke of the horror of death in combat, of peace, of the protection of the poor, of prayer and of almsgiving.

Baï engraved on Musa's heart the spirit of Islam and its sacred rites. Musa for his part learned from Baï's example and wide-ranging knowledge. His life had taken a new turning. He had become a convinced Muslim.

When he returned to the Hoggar after the defeat of his tribe, he found anarchy reigning there. There was no one to take command, apart from an aged chief. Musa realized that his hour had come. Blindly following Baï's instructions and helped by considerable political acumen, he formed the 'peace party'. He persuaded his followers to parley with the French. Nevertheless, in the style proper to a proud Touareg, he would turn his submission into a political victory.

That would happen in a few hours time. The oasis of In Salah was in sight.

They all got down from their camels. They unpacked their finest robes: the white, purple and striped *gandourahs* which are worn one over the other and tied at the waist with a strip of cloth. With the help of a mirror, each member of the party adjusted, with exactness born of practice, and with a personal touch, the long brilliant blue turbans which revealed no more than their eyes. The camels' flanks were adorned with bright-coloured rugs with long braids at the ends.

They got back into the saddle and held their spears; their daggers were attached to their arms and their swords to their belts. They would appear at the meeting-place as people of importance.

The French were there too, wearing their quaint *képis*.

They all dismounted. It was a solemn moment. As stiff and unbending as the spears which they held against them, the Touareg moved forward in line, step by step. The French also came forward, but in a group. Everyone stopped at arms-length and the usual formal greetings were exchanged, and repeated ten times:

'Blessings upon you!' began Musa.

'And upon you!' said the captain.

'How are you?'

'What news?'

'How is everyone?'

'Where has it rained?'

'Drought everywhere!'

The ceremony lasted for hours. The two parties were still suspicious of one another. But peace was made.

Musa accepted the red *burnous* with gold tassels which the French presented to the chiefs whom they nominated. For that reason it lost some of its attraction for the Touareg.

To be sure, Musa had been appointed chief by the French. But he had already imposed himself upon his own people. He had accepted the French commission, yes – but in his own way. There was no reason for anyone to be any less respectful towards him, for 'when his eye grew fiery, the heat was strong enough to cook a goat'.

The dignity of his bearing was so great that, much later, a service officer at In Salah remembered the worrying impression it made on him: 'Musa's reception . . . went beyond due bounds. The impression I still retain of his entry at In Salah was that of a triumphant warrior or a powerful sovereign. The natives . . . did not witness any public submission . . . The result is an uncomfortable sense of ambiguity which ought to be removed.'

3

The meeting at the well

25 June 1905. In a French column in the southern Hoggar, near the well of In Ouzzel.

The soldiers had slept in a square, with rifles loaded and every man on alert, because bandit groups from Morocco were scouring the countryside. There were not many men in the column. It consisted of some hastily-instructed Arab soldiers, a few French officers and five civilians. Their mission was to establish peaceful contact with the population.

The sun bore down on them fiercely. It was near 50°C (120°F) in the shade. They were drinking up to ten litres (17 pints) of water a day. This was the real desert. An interminable expanse of sand and pebbles. Here and there was a *wadi*, or dry river-bed, which the rain that year had made green and which attracted large numbers of nomads.

There was a mood of nervous expectation in the camp. A meeting with Musa had been arranged at the well of In Ouzzel. Since the meeting last year at In Salah, he had not been seen again and questions were being asked.

But everything went well. Musa appeared with the Touareg elders, and contact was soon established. They sat in a circle and discussed practical matters.

It was not long before two men were studying one another attentively.

One of them was Musa, son of Amastane. He was staring at a short man hardly 5ft 5in. tall, wearing nothing impressive, and slightly bowed. His tanned face was framed in a poorly-trimmed beard. What struck one immediately was his eyes — both penetrating and gentle. A broad mouth with many missing teeth produced a heartfelt smile, as warm as the sun at In Ouzzel. On his almost bald head he wore a kind of woollen hat fitted with a nape-guard against the sun. His white tunic was torn and too short, and held together awkwardly at the waist with a leather belt. It was like the tunics of the northern nomads. A long pair of rosary beads of heavy black wood hung from his belt. A red heart with a cross on it was sewn on his chest. [At the time, this was a sign of renewal in the Catholic Church, of a desire to restore a heart to a Church suffering from institutionalization and lack of warmth.] He wore Saharan sandals that he had made himself.

The captain performed the introductions: 'Charles de Foucauld, servant of the one God. He loves solitude and wishes to learn the language of the Kel Ahaggar'.

Musa knew that already. News travels fast in the Sahara.

Almost involuntarily, Musa compared his 'own' marabout, Baï, with the marabout of the French. He was impressed by the latter's simplicity. De Foucauld sat cross-legged beside the captain, who was seated on a folding stool. Far from trying to direct the conversation, as Baï would have done, the French marabout had decided to remain withdrawn. Far from keeping his distance and hiding his true feelings behind a mysterious expression, however, the French marabout gave all possible signs of friendliness. Musa was surprised to discover that he already spoke the language of the Touareg.

Musa's and the French marabout's first impression of one another were mixed.

De Foucauld immediately recorded in his notebook: 'Musa is a good and pious Muslim, with the ideas and way of life, qualities and disadvantages of a Muslim who acts in strict accordance with his faith but at the same time keeps as open a mind as possible'.

Musa, for his part, must certainly have wondered what a 'marabout' was doing among soldiers.

And the French marabout asked the same question: 'Will they be able to tell soldiers from priests, and see us as God's servants . . .? I don't know.'

Then came the delicate question which Musa had been afraid of. It too was posed by the captain: 'The French marabout would like to settle in the Hoggar'.

Musa knew how suspicious his people were. But how could he refuse a request from the French? They were stronger. Moreover, they seemed to trust him. But what if something happened to this marabout?

Charles de Foucauld noted down: 'With Musa's agreement it was decided that I should remain in the Hoggar'. But Musa's agreement and undertaking to ensure the marabout's safety was certainly not based on whim. He thought the matter over carefully and decided himself the exact spot where de Foucauld's dwelling was to be built.

This man with a heart sewn on his breast is the man we are looking for – Charles de Foucauld.

What was this forty-seven-year-old marabout hiding under his white robes? Why have we met him here, near the well at In Ouzzel?

Like Musa, he was a convert. To get to know him, we must follow the way he has taken to reach this point.

We shall have to leave the heat-bound Sahara for a time. Thirteen chapters later we shall meet up with Musa on the same day and at the same well.

In the meantime we shall steer for the fogs of Europe.

4
Leap into loneliness

11 April 1874. The Paris to Nancy train.

It was late. The train was shaking the travellers' heads to and fro. A very respectable grandfather was snoring gently. He had a grey moustache and beard and was wearing a black frock-coat. He sat between his two grandchildren: Charles – our future marabout – and Marie, Charles's sister.

Charles was a lad of fifteen with full-blown cheeks, a bit too fat for his age. That year he would be sitting the first part of his baccalauréat, his school-leaving examination. He looked rather lazy and indifferent, not very pleasant.

That evening especially he felt more of an orphan than ever before.

He came of an aristocratic family, and was hardly five years of age when his mother died of a miscarriage. A family drama had preceded her death. For reasons still somewhat obscure, her husband had left the household some months before the fatal miscarriage. Five months later he died as well.

Charles was a very precocious child and had certainly sensed the tensions, tears and mysterious goings-on. They had made him extremely sensitive and introverted. But from his mother he had received the first imprints of the Catholic faith.

The grandfather, a retired colonel, had undertaken the up-bringing of the two children. But how could he replace a mother?

Luckily Charles discovered a second family, his father's sister's, including his cousin Marie – who is not to be confused with his sister. They saw one another during the holidays and wrote to one another. Marie, eight years older than Charles, was a sensible and unassuming girl who did not talk needlessly and never preached. She had an unwavering faith and above all a warm heart. She became a sister, a confidante and almost a girl-friend to Charles. Later he would call her, 'Mother dear'.

In the train that evening Charles was not analyzing the way

he felt about his cousin. All he knew was that he had just been at her wedding, that she was now Madame de Bondy, and lived only for her husband.

Perhaps Charles had dreamed that she would remain his confidante, and his alone . . . In any case, that dream had gone and Charles was on his own.

God knows he needed Marie just then. Since she had become engaged to be married, he had noticed that his faith had disappeared. Not that he was a convinced atheist, but in the schools and in the spirit of the age, science and technology were the only gods. God himself could neither be weighed nor measured. Therefore he could not be reached. They were neither for nor against him. He was just a pointless subject. 'It was not that I had bad teachers', wrote Charles, 'but those I had were bad influences because they were so neutral.'

What could he hang onto? He was orphaned from his parents and orphaned from God. He had lost the only person in whom he could confide. In the midst of a world devoted to the question-mark, he felt rejected and incapable of making friends of boys or girls. He became a loner, interested only in himself.

His own body became his best friend. An unfortunate friend. Charles began to over-eat; he grew obsessed by his developing sexuality, and appallingly lazy.

After his exams, he decided to become a soldier. That was the right life for an aristocrat. He chose Saint-Cyr, the least exacting of military academies. He left it as No. 333 out of 386! In a few weeks he would be twenty.

'Despairing of truth'

'. . . at fifteen, when I lost the faith.'

'I think I have never been in so sad a state of mind. In a certain way I did much worse things on other occasions, but all the same something good occurred alongside what was bad; at seventeen I was quite egotistical, impious, longing to do evil: it was as if I had gone mad.'

'When I was doing my worst, I was convinced that that was quite in order.'

'The same faith with which so many religions are practised seemed to me to condemn them all; my childhood faith with its Three-in-One[1] seemed to me least tenable of all. I could never bring myself to accept it.'

'For twelve years I neither rejected nor believed anything; I despaired of the truth and did not even believe in God, for no proof of his existence seemed adequate.'

1 The Christian mystery of the one God who reveals himself as Father, Son and Spirit.

5

'I am a man without a future'

15 September 1878. Charles's twentieth birthday.

The family met at cousin Marie's to celebrate the occasion. Grandfather had died in February that year.

His death was a turning-point for Charles. A wish to avoid scandal, not to make his grandfather worse, had more or less forced Charles to be discreet. Now he was free. The loner became a young man at large in society, but no less of a solitary for all that. An unbelievably big inheritance was his – 840,000 gold francs in the currency of the day.

If he had been introduced to drugs, perhaps Charles would have spent his fortune on them. Escape! Escape from the emptiness which marred his life more and more. No drugs? Well then, let's spend! The anaesthesia of ultimate luxury. He could shine that way at least.

Charles still had a year at Saumur before his training as a cavalry officer would be completed. After six o'clock he was to be found in a private room at a restaurant. For three or four hours he would stay there alone sampling the finest dishes. For some time he used to have a plate of pâté de foie gras with truffles at his bedside. At night all he had to do was to stretch out his hand without opening his eyes.

He always dressed in the latest fashion and had his hairdresser come to the house. He never allowed a waiter to give him change from a gold coin. Sometimes he did not bother to collect his salary.

The room he shared with a companion at the barracks became famous for the splendid dinners and extended card parties which took place there in order to keep whoever was under sentence company – it was unusual for one of them not to be under arrest. If Foucauld won too much he would pretend to lose. His dry humour was appreciated, as were his neat jokes . . . and above all his purse.

Later, in the barracks he liked to entertain in small groups, without showing any favouritism. At that time he kept small but comfortable lodgings in the town. He had a servant, an English carriage and a horse.

As if all that were not enough, he also gave superb dinners in a very attractive, small, old style *hôtel* which he owned in Nancy.

What was the result? He became increasingly obese and passed out of the cavalry school at Saumur eighty-seventh out of eighty-seven.

From then on he led a monotonous garrison life that ended in Algeria.

Like a drug-addict who does everything to get his next 'fix', Charles did everything to stay in his dream-world. He was afraid of running into reality – the empty hopelessness of his life. His round of pleasure became all but neurotic. Until the day when he went too far.

He had taken his mistress, Mimi, to Algeria, and tried to pass her off as the 'Viscountess de Foucauld'. Fate had it that she was accepted as such by the local officers. When the deception was uncovered his gallant colleagues forced him into a corner: the woman or the army.

Charles chose Mimi. Nevertheless she would seem to have been no more than an object of pleasure for him. Did he ever love a woman? No one knows.

He refused to obey the ultimatum because it was unacceptable to him that anyone should interfere in his private life. He lost his commission for 'lack of discipline, together with publicly unbecoming conduct'.

He was twenty-two. He returned to Europe and set himself up with Mimi in Switzerland. 'I am a man without a future.'

He stayed in Switzerland no more than two and a half months.

The two faces of a play-boy

'Look, old friend, after a good meal there is nothing better than a good cigar and a good low-slung carriage to take you home, so that you do not have to lift your feet too high in the air when getting in.'

To a girl who cried on finding herself abandoned so quickly: 'How do you think I could attach myself to anyone, since I find you all equally sweet and attractive?'

'You, Lord, allowed me to feel a painful emptiness, a sadness that I have never experienced until this moment. It returned each evening when I found myself alone in my flat . . . It made me dumb and depressed during so-called celebrations: I organized them, but when the time came I let them pass over me, dumb, uninterested, and infinitely bored.'

'. . . since then I have been surrounded by darkness, and there is nothing left for me. I have only myself now. That is, absolute egotism in darkness and filth . . . Those who had tasted worldly pleasures to the full thought nothing of me . . . I disgusted them . . . I was not so much a man as a swine.'

6
'I won through'

Beginning of July 1881. Algeria. In the heat of battle.

In this corner of the Sahara, now in a state of insurrection, the former Charles was unrecognizable. He marched and thirsted with the soldiers. He shared dangers with them. Like them he slept on the ground. He was here, there and everywhere, in the thick of it all. His men worshipped him. He was a leader and enjoyed leading.

What had happened?

He had begun to take an interest in French colonial politics. Tunisia was to become a French protectorate. Charles's regiment was to be posted there. Perhaps this was an opportunity to shine as never before? The idea of military service developed again.

The following note he made still holds its secret: 'Something good had broken through alongside the bad'.

Then the sudden news! Four companies from his regiment were sent to put down an Algerian rebellion. This was the drop of water which filled the barrel to overflowing . . .

He made a quick decision and was taken back into the army. It was to be Algeria, not Tunisia.

Goodbye the good times! Goodbye Mimi!

A young twenty-three-year-old seemed to have found his place again among other men.

The rebels were squashed. But they had made Charles curious and awakened in this loner an irresistible desire to get to know other people, to know the unknown. Real human relations – that was what had been missing in his life.

Charles learned Arabic and read the Koran. He asked the army for an opportunity to study the subject nation. The army refused. Charles left again and changed his plans. He decided on a long trip of exploration through Morocco. He was sent by the French Geographical Society.

The risk was considerable, suicidal. Two Europeans travelling through Morocco at the same time disappeared. His family tried to dissuade him. In vain. From Morocco, Charles wrote later to his sister: 'If one leaves saying that one is going to do something, one must not return without having done it'.

A year later a Jewish rabbi was travelling deep in Morocco. He wore a shirt with trailing sleeves, trousers cut off at the knees, a dark cloth waistcoat, and a woollen robe with a hood and enormous sleeves. On his head he had a black cap and wore prayer-locks. On his shoulder was a goat-hair bag. When he entered a town he took off his sandals. Like all Jews he was forced to go barefoot.

A Jewish rabbi? No, it was Foucauld! This disguise was the only means by which he could hope to avoid drawing attention to himself.

He had been walking all day. 'I always had a notebook five centimetres square hidden in my left hand. I used a stub of pencil, which I never left out of my other hand, to write down what I saw on either side . . . In that way I was almost always writing as I went along . . . I was careful enough to walk in front of or behind my companions, so that with the aid of my capacious garments they would not notice the slight movements of my hands. The contempt in which Jews were held helped my isolation . . . Night-time once again brought solitude and work'.

The appalling smell of the ghetto was unbearable. The worst things of all for Foucauld were the lice, bugs and fleas in the worn-out mattresses of the ordinary houses. He would never get used to lice.

Nevertheless Charles discovered the sacred law of hospitality among Muslims as well as Jews. It was something entirely new to him. He loved it. Up to then Muslims had been 'the enemy'. Now he met them as friends.

He had hardly arrived in one town when the leading Muslims grew curious about the Jew from so far away and invited him in. Now and then some hosts sensed who he really was. They made smiling allusions and offered gifts most civilly. One of them even risked his life for Charles. 'From then on my relationship with him was that of a friend. I exchanged trust for trust . . . I told him clearly who I was . . . His friendship was all the more secure.'

The danger was very great on three occasions. And each time

a Muslim risked everything to save Charles. The third time he almost lost his life. Luckily he was only a few days from the Algerian border, which was under French control.

Without a penny in his pocket, exhausted, he introduced himself to the duty officer. For a year he had been used to greeting others humbly, and so he began by bowing. Realizing that a different bearing was more suitable, he straightened himself up proudly and rapped out: 'Lieutenant de Foucauld, returning from Morocco!' The poor officer was quite taken aback.

Charles told a friend: 'It was tough but interesting, and I won through'.

Foucauld had emerged from his shell. He had his fellow officers to thank for that. – But also the friendship and co-operation of Muslims and Jews.

Now he was twenty-five. He would never forget Morocco.

7

In a trice

For three full years after leaving Morocco, de Foucauld was wholly taken up with the work for his sizeable book *A Journey through Morocco*.

In addition he met with an extraordinary inward adventure.

Imagine a pair of dancers moving gracefully over the dance-floor. One of the partners is dancing quite different steps and is supported by an invisible partner! Until . . . No! Let Charles tell his own story.[1]

On 23 May 1884 he left Morocco. 'Islam has had a profound effect on me . . . Acquaintance with this faith . . . has allowed me to sense something much bigger and more true than worldly preoccupations . . . I began to study Islam'. And he went so far as to say: 'I have thought of becoming a Muslim.'

Charles thought of staying in Algeria. 'When I came back from Morocco I was no better than a few years before and my first visit to Algeria had been full of bad things.'

Exhausted and depressed, he left for France where he could find some rest with his family. He appreciated 'solitude together with those one loves most in the world'.

He met his cousin Marie again. As he wrote in a letter to her: 'You have been so kind . . . that once again I began to see and to realize the good that had been forgotten for the space of ten years. And the year which followed was a little less hateful than the previous ones'.

At the end of 1884 he became engaged to be married in Algeria. He told his future wife: 'As for me, I shall not be a practising Catholic as I do not believe'. In December he broke the engagement.

Two years later, in February 1886, he settled in Paris, not far from his aunt and his cousin Marie.

'You inspired them to accept me as the long-lost son whom

[1] The following passages were written some years after the events.

they never allowed to feel that he had ever left his father's house.' 'My cousin helped with her discretion, kindness, gentle nature . . . but she did not act directly.'

'My heart and my spirit remained a long way from you, yet I lived in a less vicious atmosphere. It was neither the light nor the goodness, far from it, but the filth was not so deep.'

'Now I found chastity attractive, my heart required it'.

In the same February of 1886 he had his first meeting in Paris with the well-known priest Huvelin. His church was only a few steps away from Charles's flat.

'You allowed me to look for pagan virtue in the books of the pagan philosophers, and I found only emptiness and disgust.'

'I did not believe that people could recognize truth.'

He commented on a book given him by his cousin: 'It made me see that perhaps the Christian religion was true'.

'You are continually at work in my soul . . . You transform it with absolute power and astonishing speed, and it quite ignores You'.

On seeing his cousin Marie, he thought: 'Because she is so intelligent, the religion she so strongly believes in cannot be as mad as I thought.'

Towards the end of the same year: 'I began to go to church but without believing, for it was only there that I felt right and spent hours saying the same prayer: "My God, if You exist, let me recognize You".

'At the beginning of October 1886, after six months spent with my family, I admired and wanted virtue, but I did not know You.'

On 28 or 29 October 1886, he said to his cousin: 'You are happy to believe; I am looking for the light and I cannot find it'.

On the very next day, he went to see Father Huvelin in the church of St Augustine. 'I asked for religious instruction. He made me kneel down and make my confession and sent me to take communion at once.'

In a trice his dancing-partner had taken the initiative.

'As soon as I believed that there was a God, I understood that I could not do anything other than live for him. My religious vocation dates from the same moment as my faith. God is so great!'

Charles was then twenty-eight years of age. He said not a word to anyone about his conversion. Even he, usually so exact about dates, could not remember the precise day. The direct encounter with his Partner had really taken Charles by surprise.

'At first faith had many obstacles to overcome. I had doubted so very much that I did not believe everything all at once . . . For instance, I would find the Gospel miracles incredible, or try to mix passages from the Koran with my Christian prayers.'

The countenance of the mysterious Partner in the dance remains invisible to us. All that we sense of Him is that strong hand which had started to guide Charles on the right way.

For him, the dance had only just begun.

8

The unknown takes shape

10 January 1889. On the way to Nazareth.

Two long years had already passed since the great meeting. Twenty days ago Charles had begun a pilgrimage on horseback through the Holy Land. He looked imposing with his expressive eyes, well-tended moustache, and the distinguished manners of a nobleman.

On his way from the hill of the Beatitudes, he was approaching Nazareth.

'Jesus' eyes had rested on the same mountains, the same hills, the same sights which my eyes now contemplated.'

After a half-hour's climb Nazareth, still a little way off, came into sight. It was a little town, lacking in charm. Dotted with church-towers and cypresses, it was built at different levels among the rocks. The great majority of the eight to ten thousand inhabitants were Christians.

Charles almost certainly visited the different churches in Nazareth. He was taken to the grotto naively described as the dwelling-place of Jesus and his family.

But the historical error is of no importance. Charles was in a strange state of inward recollection. It was a condition that he would hardly ever experience again in his life. It was as if he were unconscious.

He turned into a narrow alleyway in the Muslim quarter. The boxlike houses certainly had not changed much since Jesus' time. Several craftsmen were at work before their doors. For the most part they were making ploughs. Even their gestures were those of their predecessors of centuries before. They stretched out their legs and used their naked toes to hold still the pieces of wood they were working.

The rhythm of the blacksmiths' hammers joined the songs of the artisans. It was quite easy to think oneself no longer with Charles de Foucauld in the year 1889 but transported to the beginning of our era and the Nazareth of Jesus Christ himself.

'To have spent so many moments in this dwelling-place of Nazareth in which he lived for thirty years . . . to have reached the place where his voice resounded for so long . . . to have walked along the streets which he traversed every day as a poor artisan . . . All that and everything else were exceptional graces which it is impossible to express; above all they were gifts which left an ineradicable impression.'

Everything was in turmoil in Charles' sensitive heart. Or, rather, he was bemused by the changing precision and imprecision of two so-to-speak superimposed cinematic images: that of the 'God is so great!' of Charles's conversion and that of the 'God is so small!' of Nazareth.

An astonishing image coalesced. Foucauld, dumb and lost in thought, was seized by the sharp image of the Face which now invaded the screen. 'God is so great!' and 'God is so small!' now fitted perfectly together. They had become the 'Workman God of Nazareth'.

Charles realized what still had to be done. 'I do not want to spend my time journeying through life in a first-class carriage when the One whom I love went through it in the lowest class.'

He returned to France. A year later, on 15 January 1890, he abandoned everything in order to become a monk. After a few months in a monastery in France, he entered a poor monastery in the East. He said goodbye to his cousin Marie.

'At that time, at five o'clock, I was close to you again, and for the last time in this world . . . The time! How I remember your watch which ticked away my last minutes . . .' When he left he was in tears.

The next day he wrote to her: 'I cannot get used to the idea that I have said farewell to you for ever . . . and that my eyes will never see yours again'.

Did Charles take his place on the open upstairs deck of a bus (where the poorer passengers sat at that time), as some people claim they saw him do at this stage of his life?

'Blessed are the poor: that is the beatitude that I am looking for.'

Charles was thirty-one years of age.

How quickly he makes himself poor

Lord Jesus, how quickly he who loves you with his whole heart
makes himself poor
and cannot bear
to be richer than his Beloved . . .

My God,
I do not know how it is possible
for some to see you in poverty
and themselves voluntarily to stay rich . . .
I cannot understand a love
without a need, a compelling need
to imitate,
to resemble
the Beloved,
and above all to share
all his pains,
all his difficulties,
and all the burdens of his life.

To be rich . . .
to live in comfort among my possessions
while you were so poor and in such need
and living in misery
under the burden of harsh labour,
I just could not do it,
O God . . .
I could not love like that.

(Written in Nazareth eight years later)

9

Between flute and violins

9 July 1890. Charles disembarks in Syria.

The next day he arrived at the little monastery of Akbes, which stood in a remote valley. Some twenty monks lived there, in a 'group of thatched huts built from wooden planks and mud . . . cooped up together out of fear of attacks and of robbers'.

'Since I have been here, I have spent two or three days a week . . . washing, and the remainder working in the fields,' when it was not necessary to cut wood. A very strict framework of about six hours of prayer alternated with manual labour. Everything was framed in perpetual silence.

Charles had become a monk. 'Out of love, out of love.' He believed he was keeping in step with his divine Partner. 'Everyone knows that the first effect of love is imitation. Therefore I had still to enter the Order in which I would find the closest imitation of Jesus . . . the poor and humble workman of Nazareth.'

He would make a public promise to dedicate his life to his community.

But, believe it or not, he soon realized that he had made a mistake. The life of the poor, humble workman of Nazareth and the life of a monastery were two different things.

Four months after his arrival he wrote: 'We are poor in the eyes of the rich, but not so poor as our Lord was, not so poor as I was in Morocco'.

Obviously Charles needed a life in sharp contrast to his past. But above all he bore the mark of the Carpenter of Nazareth, that 'thirst at last to lead the life which . . . I had foreseen . . . when walking the streets of Nazareth . . . I had thought that I would find it in . . . this monastery . . . but from the start I saw that this was not the case'.

Huvelin, who remained Charles's adviser for many years, was upset, but eventually accepted this change of course: 'In fact I do not think that you can resist this impulse'.

Although Charles was totally unfitted for community life, his relations with individual brothers were good. They respected him. But the wisest of his brethren wrote: 'He is always edifying, often a source of joy, and sometimes frightening'.

In fact Charles found it difficult to practise brotherly love. Though he loved his brothers, he criticized his community. Blinded by his own vocation, he was sometimes hard or unjust: 'There is so little love for Holy Poverty around me . . . they are so little desirous of following our Lord . . . that I sometimes fear . . . that I shall lose any respect for the people around me'. 'I can see a worldly spirit has settled among us all.'

How certain Charles had been when he entered the monastic life! Three years later, he was up in arms against obedience. He was not by nature a man who could easily adapt himself. When it was a question of his vocation, everything became complicated.

He wrote to his cousin Marie: 'You know too that . . . I often – or at least sometimes – find obedience towards my superiors difficult . . . When one has received certain orders tending in a direction which is not what one would wish, or at least what I do not want, I am strongly tempted to defy my superiors'. 'It is not that I don't like obedience, but I don't want to put obedience to men before obedience to God.'

This was no theoretical problem. Charles had it in mind to found a new religious order: the Little Brothers. Nothing less than that! Its goal would be to 'imitate the hidden life of our Lord at Nazareth' . . . The rule was ready, although still quite new. It was as splendid as it was quite unlivable!

Huvelin and Charles's superiors were dumbfounded. They were afraid that he might be going insane. He was already tense enough. Huvelin begged him not to 'think of gathering people round you, *and especially not of giving them a rule*'.

If he had still been in the army, Charles would soon have settled things. No agreement? Right, goodbye!

But he remained a monk, for seven and a half years in fact, torn between what he thought of as two obediences: to God and to man.

It was as if he were dancing away, trying to keep up with an orchestra's demands. One movement took him close to the flutes: 'Everything within me says that I should give into my wishes'. The next took him close to the violins: 'My father [his superior] tells me to wait . . . what really keeps me back is obedience'. Then it was the flutes again: 'Every day I see more clearly that I am just not at home here'.

Charles was slowly learning an important lesson of life: the divine Partner does not act alone.

It was He who was secretly whispering in his heart, as he followed the flute. It was He who sounded through human voices like the moving forest of bows on violins.

If you listen only to the flutes, you cannot hear the symphony. There was no question of dancing alone. What Charles wanted was to dance with Another. 'Obedience is the consummation of love.'

Seven and a half years, then, were to pass before the voice of men and the sound of the flute were heard in unison. Eventually the superior-general of the Order advised Charles to follow his impulse. It was time: 'My soul was truly sick . . .'

Charles was thirty-eight years of age. He left. 'And now the unknown was before me.'

10
A scrap of bread

9 March 1897. Nazareth, in front of a poor convent.

The bell rang. The sister who opened the door was rather taken aback. Here he was again, that odd fellow! Three days before he had stayed all day long, praying in the tiny convent chapel. His clothes had made some women laugh.

They had good reason. Charles – for that is who it was – wore a long blue-and-white striped, hooded garment with a white woollen cap on his head, around which he had wrapped a kind of turban. He also had on a pair of blue workman's trousers and sandals, and of course there were immense rosary beads hanging from his leather belt. His only luggage was a small notebook with the four Gospels written out in his own hand.

The stranger wanted to speak to the Mother Superior.

Charles was exhausted. He had just repeated, but on foot, the pilgrimage he made on horseback eight years ago. A twelve days' beard replaced the well-kept moustache of that trip. He had begged his bread on the way.

But here was the Mother Superior. She had been told discreetly that the stranger was to be taken seriously.

Charles tried to appear a bit of a simpleton. He even used a few rather rough expressions, for fear of being recognized. But he was a bad actor. 'He wanted to be a servant. He didn't want any wages. All the food he wanted was bread and water. He especially wanted enough time for prayer.'

The Mother Superior decided to take the risk. She offered Charles the gardener's lodging. Charles refused. He would rather have the wooden hut he had just noticed. It looked like a sentry-box.

They rustled up two trestles, two planks, a straw mattress and a kind of thick coverlet. A table and a stool completed the dwelling. And of course there was the stone which would serve as his pillow and the mat which would replace the mattress.

The first work he was given was to rebuild a fence. Poor fence!

It was not long before the sisters realized that their mysterious servant had hands fitted more to drawing than to carpentry or masonry. The result was that, apart from a little handiwork and seeing to the post, Charles's only work consisted in drawing pious pictures for the sisters. After that he could do what he liked.

What then was the meaning of Charles's remarks about imitating God, the workman of Nazareth, and taking his place in the poorest class?

'I infinitely rejoiced to be poor, clothed like a workman, a servant, in the lowly state which Jesus our Lord enjoyed'. 'God . . . you made yourself the least of men . . . you came down among them in order to . . . live the life of a poor worker.' 'As for me, I shall always look for the lowest place.'

Was Charles in his right mind when he talked about leading a workman's life? What are we to think of a workman who spent his days drawing, reading and praying?

Our dreamer was to spend three years thus before he opened his eyes: 'My situation here certainly has something false about it . . . I work, but my work isn't really work'.

In fact, in three years' time he would have left Nazareth, where he felt he was becoming 'as snug as a bug in a rug'.

And what about his remarks on taking the lowest place? Did Jesus really occupy the least of all places because he was a carpenter: Charles's notions were those we would expect from a French aristocrat of the period.

Nevertheless it was a real descent for him. Between the viscount with a fine moustache and the 'sisters' servant' collecting dung in the Nazareth gutters, there was a considerable difference. On the other hand, he had not quite found the least of all places, which he had known in Morocco.

At Nazareth the sisters eventually learned about his past, his conversion, and his rank. He became the centre of a kind of quiet veneration.

Jesus himself had spoken of the lowest place in connection with a banquet. The lowest place? Surely that was the worker's place? The place of the slave of the new tyrant whose name was CAPITAL? As an eye-witness of the period says: 'You should see them arriving every morning! There are many women among them, pale, thin, walking barefoot in the mud. When it rains they wear their apron or dress on their heads. There is an even greater number of young children, dirty, ragged, and greasy from the oil that dropped on them from the looms while they tended them. The scraps of bread that are to keep them alive until nightfall they carry in their hands or hide in their clothes'.

What about these children? Charles de Foucauld had never seen them close to. He was completely ignorant of their way and condition of life. But a fierce impulse told him to 'descend'. He was not wrong.

Every morning Charles carried his jug of water and his basket to the convent. In it the sisters put the scrap of bread that would last him for the day.

A scrap of bread . . . the same scrap of bread that the factory children had to content themselves with.

A strange encounter. Without even knowing it, following Jesus brings one close to the humblest of all.

11
The secret key

1897–1900. Nazareth.

Every love story has its secrets. It was night-time. Charles carried a lantern and was walking toward the convent. He took the key from his pocket. The Mother Superior had let him have it in great secrecy. The sisters knew nothing about it.

Charles opened the chapel door. He went to his usual place. He went down on his knees and looked straight at the Tabernacle where the Blessed Sacrament was. The long struggle against boredom and sleep was beginning.

As far as he could, Charles changed his position to ensure that he stayed awake. On his knees, standing, sometimes with his head resting on the top of the pew. Was he going to sleep? He sat down. He took out his notebook and opened the Gospel. He forced himself to write down his thoughts. 'These are often prayers, intimate conversations . . . I tell Him everything that I have to tell Him, we are very close'.

In the daytime it was more or less the same. Charles wrote humorously that he left it to his good angel to wake him up, for he had no watch. He estimated that he slept about five-and-a-half hours. He began the day with matins, a sequence of psalms, Biblical readings and prayers, in his hut. Then he meditated by writing on a biblical text before he went to the convent chapel to hear mass with the nuns.

Sometimes they saw him arriving with big books under his arm: the Bible, the works of his favourite saints, and books of theology which he read 'at the feet of the One of whom they speak'.

'All these readings are dear to me, but I make them short. Then I profit all the more from them, and that leaves me most of my time for prayer . . . trying to contemplate Him always.'

What a difference from his life in the monastery in Syria.

There the precise timetable and the far too long vocal prayers had ruled his life. Manual labour sometimes cut into the time

set aside for prayer. It was a strict community life for which
Charles was not made.

Here it was love at first sight. Charles could stay as he wished
at the feet of the Carpenter whom he had met in his native town
of Nazareth.

'Jesus and Jesus alone, without anything else, just Jesus.'
'Let us accept the Gospel . . . for it is according to the Gospel
that we shall be judged.' 'Your rule: Follow me . . . It is Your
only rule, but it is Your absolute rule.'

Nothing surprising about such simplicity. After all it was a
love story, and love stories are eminently simple.

Was any other proof needed? After three years in Nazareth,
Charles went to France to prepare for ordination to the priesthood. He came upon one of the pearls of the Bible, the Song of
Songs. The ecstatic declarations of two lovers which express the
love of God for his people. As a book of poetry, it rings so true
that at that time of strong taboos it seemed a rather ambiguous
book to have in the Bible.

Charles copied out no less than forty-two passages from this
poem which takes up only about four pages in most Bibles.

> *'Let him kiss me with the kisses of his mouth.*
> *A bundle of myrrh is my well-beloved unto me;*
> *he shall lie all night betwixt my breasts.*
> *Thou hast ravished my heart, my sister, my spouse,*
> *thou hast ravished my heart with one of thy looks,*
> *with one of the locks which hang on thy neck.'*

(Passages copied by Charles de Foucauld)

It did not really matter that Charles grew bored and fell asleep
in front of the Tabernacle. He was waiting, like all lovers! Here
undoubtedly we have the secret key to his enterprise.

The two faces of a lover

'The best prayer is the one with the most love in it.'

'Rejoice to know that God is God.'

'As soon as you are in love, you must want to be close to your beloved.'

Of Father Huvelin: 'He turns religion into love'.

His vow of celibacy: 'The symbol of an ever-youthful love'.

'Adoration . . . this dumb admiration which comprises the most passionate declaration of love.'

*   *

'I find everything difficult . . . communion, prayer . . . everything, even telling Jesus that I love him . . . I have to cling on to the life of faith. If only I felt that Jesus loved me. But he never says so.'

'Before the Blessed Sacrament . . . everything seems empty, hollow, meaningless, except for the fact that I am at the feet of our Lord, contemplating him . . . and when I am at his feet, I am dry, arid, without a word or a thought, and often, alas, I end up by going to sleep.'

'At least four evenings in a row I have gone to sleep while writing down these little meditations.'

12
The Gospel at the end of a pen

1897–1901. Three years at Nazareth and one in France.

The pen and the pencil were the real tools of Charles de Foucauld. With his fine writing he covered notebooks, exercise books, writing paper, used envelopes, printed family letters announcing births, marriages, and so on.

Charles, the man of action, found it 'so impossible to pray' that he wrote to stop himself sleeping or dreaming.

At the beginning, it poured out like a novel. As time passed, he became more selective. The texts grew shorter. The whole thing lasted less than two years. In that time – in addition to other things – he must have filled some 1500 pages with meditations on the Gospel.

A year-and-a-half later, when preparing for ordination to the priesthood, he contented himself with copying Bible passages which had impressed and influenced him. A few years later, nothing. He no longer had enough time.

Three-quarters of all the 'spiritual writings' of Charles de Foucauld date from these two years of his life. We must not forget that.

The most striking aspect of these texts is the importance of the Bible for Charles de Foucauld. At that time this was not customary among Catholics. Two-thirds of all the spiritual writings of the whole of his life are biblical.

Another impressive feature is the almost childlike simplicity of his style. There is no need to be a theologian to understand what he has to say. How rare that is!

Some passages in his writings are marvellous sleeping pills! Others are calculated to make one smile. Some seem too contrived and sentimental, and the pious style of the period shows through. Many texts seem to have no connection with life as actually lived. Others appear exaggerated, too extreme. But, here and there, there is a pearl which is worth all the rest.

Everything seems false, of course, if we forget the goal of his writings. A lover has to remain awake during prayer; the style is that of love letters. There is a lot of repetition. There are some silly things. The heart alone is talking. These texts are valuable only by virtue of the love which dictates them.

At the beginning of June 1901 Charles ended his retreat in preparation for ordination. He had an inspiration. At one go, he delved into his memory for his thirty favourite gospel texts. There, at the end of his pen, we sense something of his attitude to Jesus.

Perhaps the two pages which follow are worth lingering over . . .

Father, into your hands I commend my spirit.
Follow me.
Jesus.
I have come to bring fire upon the earth.
To save what was lost.
To enlighten those who were in darkness and in the shadow of death.
To give captives their freedom and the blind their sight.
I am the good shepherd.
Who among you would not leave the ninety-nine others (lambs?) in the wilderness to go after the one that is lost?
It is not the healthy who need medicine but the sick.
He had compassion on them because they were like sheep without a shepherd.
I have other sheep who are not in this sheepfold. I must fetch them too.
So that they may be one as We are one.
So that all may be one, so that they may be one in us.
Go out to the whole world and preach the Gospel to all people.
Teach all nations, baptizing them . . . teaching them always to do all that I have commanded you to do.
I am the way, the truth and the life. No one comes to the Father unless it is by me.

If you do not eat the flesh of the Son of man, you have no life in you.

One of the soldiers pierced his side.

Here is your mother.

As my father has sent me, I send you.

To serve and to give his life.

The good shepherd gives his life for his sheep.

I send you like lambs among wolves.

Neither silver, nor money . . . Neither possessions nor two coats.

Anyone of you who does not give up all that he owns cannot be my disciple.

They will deliver you up to death, but do not be afraid . . . Whoever acknowledges me, I shall acknowledge.

Whatever you want people to do to you, do to them.

Whenever you have done anything for one of these little brethren of mine, you have done it for me.

This is my commandment, that you love one another, as I have loved you.

There is no greater love than that a man should give his life for his friends.

(Written down from memory of the Vulgate, or Latin, text)

13
The great turning-point

16 August 1900. In sight of Marseilles.

For nine days a shabby-looking man had known what it was like to be jammed among all the others on the fourth-class deck. He was on board the ship which plied between Palestine and Marseilles. At his feet stood a little basket with his things in. He was Charles de Foucauld.

Three years in the Holy Land! And then, in the last few months, impatience, decisions, orders and counter-orders had come tumbling out together. Eventually Charles had taken the next boat.

He was well aware of the step he had taken. He tried to rehearse the strong motives which had persuaded him to return to France.

Even when he was at the monastery of Akbes in Syria, in the middle of the persecution of the Armenians, 'I wanted to be a priest and to be able to go from village to village, encouraging the Christians to die for their God'.

Hardly a year after his arrival at Nazareth, he told Father Huvelin that he wanted to be a priest. In three pages he repeated eleven times the expressions 'work' and 'do good', and underlined them.

Then he invented the famous sayings which became the leitmotif of his life: 'It is part of your vocation to proclaim the Gospel from the rooftops, not through your words but through your life'.

'I want to be a gospel worker.'

The 'Little Brothers' he wanted to found, were to be established among non-Christians. He wanted to be a priest to ensure that his first 'little fraternity' would have the Eucharist.

To Charles everything now seemed as clear as crystal. As soon as he had disembarked in France, he made his way to the monastery of Our Lady of the Snows. He spent almost a year there preparing for the priesthood. He led the same lonely life as at Nazareth. Then he would return to somewhere in the East. Yes, but . . .

A month before he was ordained priest, Charles copied down two explosive verses from the Gospel: 'I have come to bring fire upon the earth' and 'To save what was lost'.

This is the great turning-point: 'This life of *Nazareth* . . . was to be led elsewhere than in the Holy Land . . . This divine banquet whose minister I was to become, had to be offered . . . to the lame, blind, and poor, to people, that is, without priests . . . In Morocco . . . with ten million inhabitants, there was not a single priest'.

In Morocco! A thought that was not far from his heart. 'The breath of the Spirit is to be followed in all simplicity of heart'. Morocco! The only corner of the earth where Charles really learned how the poor and non-Christians lived.

Huvelin hesitated. Eventually, he relaxed the reins: 'Something stronger was driving him'. He added: 'It needed a very, bright light to show him that the right way for him was an apostolate sustained by prayer'.

Now it was up to Charles to determine 'from events' the rhythm of the next dance.

He became a priest on 9 June 1901 and left for Algeria on 9 September. He was forty-two years of age.

The heavy heat of the end of summer hung over the city of Algiers. In the drawing-room of the Lacroix family two friends were bent over staff maps: Charles and Major Lacroix. Foucauld needed Lacroix in order to obtain special permission from the governor-general to reside in the Sahara territory.

The conversation went on. They talked again about Morocco, military plans, and so on. Charles's interest was awakened. The explorer reappeared in the hermit monk from Nazareth. Only God knew, however, if the dazzling light of his recent great encounter had really made him break with the past. To the point, that is, of forgetting that Foucauld was Foucauld.

A few weeks later Charles had got all his papers together and in his pockets. He took the little train which would carry him to the edge of the desert. On the way there he made his final choice: the magnificent oasis of Beni Abbes, on the border of forbidden Morocco. Only eight months ago it had been conquered by the French.

'I wanted to travel as a poor monk.' On foot and with a donkey to carry his things.

No question of that! He was hardly off the train when he was welcomed at each post with military honours. Muslims kissed his robes. He shared the officers' table. He had to spend the night in their quarters even if he did not sleep in a bed. He discussed everything with them. That certain air of a converted man of the world that he had about him made him more sympathetic. They got a horse and a military escort ready for him.

How could he refuse without wounding them? Perhaps he had returned to the old comradeship of the Saharan soldiery? He thought that he had resigned his commission in Nazareth. But had that really killed the soldier in him? That remained to be seen.

In any case, Foucauld had been transferred directly to the complexity of the colonial world and Islam. What is more, he had been brought face to face with his alter ego. He would have to learn to understand himself.

14

Foucauld face-to-face with himself

1 December 1901. Beni Abbes.

Charles was a happy man. He had just occupied the mud house which some well-meaning soldiers had built for him within reach of the oasis but in a lonely spot. It was the 'most favourable place to start the venture, the point from which it was easiest to enter Morocco for the purpose of evangelization'.

Hardly six months after his arrival, Charles sent his friend Major Lacroix in Algiers his ideas on the reorganization of the area. The centre was to be an oasis situated right inside Moroccan territory. A short military incursion, without any blood-letting, would be enough to achieve this.

Nine months later, a group of French priests asked Charles to send them a few lines so that they could extend their petitions to cover more people. He replied with a 'missionary project for Morocco'. At the very time when the French government was expelling the religious orders from France, Charles was thinking of an invasion of Morocco by priests and religious: a first wave of contemplatives, a second wave of teaching orders and evangelizers. He himself would be in the front line!

It was all very simple. He was like a general looking over his map. Only at the end of the plan did Charles come down to earth: 'I am alone'.

More even than the evangelization of Morocco, one problem preoccupied him excessively: slavery.

'Too much work . . . a beating every day, no food or clothing, and if they try to get away . . . they are pursued with guns; and, if they are taken alive, they are mutilated . . . both their legs are crippled.' 'Almost all of them are children who have been kidnapped.' 'They were snatched away at the age of five, ten or fifteen.'

Three months after his arrival in Beni Abbes, Foucauld was pressing ahead. He wrote to his bishop: 'Slavery is kept going *on the orders of* General Risbourg . . . If there is any possibility of interventions in the Lower or Upper House of Parliament, by Catholic deputies or senators . . . let me know what should be done'.

To a friend he indignantly wrote the following: 'We have to say: "Beware, you hypocrites," you who print on your postage stamps, "Liberty, equality and fraternity", and yet manacle the slaves; you who punish the theft of a chicken and yet allow men to be kidnapped . . . we have no right to be "sleeping sentinels", "dumb dogs" . . . it is JESUS who is in this shocking condition'.

Was he right? His feelings are easy to understand. But was his strategy right? His emotion was so strong that it made him forget that missionaries risked expulsion from France under the French government laws which were tantamount to persecution of the Church. And already some of the owners of eight slaves whom Charles had rescued one by one had been to the officers to protest.

The affair would probably reach other ears higher up.

The bishop – a good man and a good friend – wanted to avoid the worst. He advised Charles to keep quiet.

Charles answered him quite sharply: 'These reasons do not leave me . . . without regretting that the representatives of Jesus are content to defend pusillanimously, but never from the roof-tops, a cause which is the cause of justice and charity'.

Two years later, he recognized that: 'By general agreement the chiefs . . . of the oasis have taken measures to suppress slavery: not in a single day – that would not be wise – but bit by bit'.

At the same time, he sent another report to the same bishop. Now it was a list of all the personnel who he thought were necessary for what had to be done at Beni Abbes: for slaves, poor travellers, the sick and old people who had been abandoned; for the Christian education of the young, two hospitals and social assistance for the poor. He had thought of everything – except that the bishop had no one to send him.

Other projects concerned 'the minute Christianity of Beni Abbes'. Even a magnifying-glass did not reveal this minute degree of Christianity in Beni Abbes. There were a few re-deemed slaves who (without enthusiasm) were subjected to first steps in Christian instruction. Charles demanded strict en-closure for them. One by one they left.

Charles was too hasty and lacked experience. But he was not wrong to express his deep apostolic longings. 'To be all to all with a unique desire in one's heart – to bring Jesus to people.'

'In order to spread the Gospel I am ready to go to the ends of the earth, and to live to the Last Judgment.'

'The grain of wheat bears fruit only when it dies.'

1 December 1901. The first mass in the chapel at Beni Abbes. Fifteen years had passed since Charles's conversion. Fifteen years later, he would die.

Fifteen years . . . that was the length of time left for the divine Partner to fit this complex man to his own rhythm. A dreamer and a pedant, humble and dominant, tender and fierce, he was a mixture of religion and politics. An individualist and pig-headed, obsessed with thoughts of action and the absolute, he was still a novice apostle.

The dance promises to be fascinating.

15
Has the Partner got lice?

1902–1903. Beni Abbes.

The sun had hardly opened an eye behind the vast orange backcloth of sand dunes. Someone was beating hard on the door to summon the marabout. He had just finished celebrating mass. He only had time to leave the Lord in his chapel to go and find Him at the door. 'Even though I get up so early, I am summoned three or four times during the period of thanksgiving at the end of the Mass.'

'From 4.30 in the morning to 8.30 in the evening I never stop talking and seeing people: slaves, the sick, soldiers, travellers, the curious.' 'Slaves fill my little house . . . the travellers come straight to the fraternity.' 'Every day there are guests to sup, sleep, breakfast . . . I have between sixty and a hundred visits a day.'

'Three or four slaves a day come here to eat. I give them bread or dates. They eat in the courtyard of the fraternity, and then they go. The guests do their own cooking. I provide barley, salt, cooking utensils.'

'I do what I can for the sick . . . whenever anyone is seriously ill, I go to see him every day.'

The fraternity even became a kindergarten. There was a three-year-old, 'Abd-Jesu, whom I have to keep by me all the time because there is no one to whom I can entrust him, even for a minute'.

What was driving this former hermit? 'I want to get all the inhabitants, Christians, Muslims, Jews and pagans, to look on me as their brother, their universal brother. They are beginning to call the house "the fraternity".' 'I chose this name to show that I am their brother, and the brother of all human beings without exception or distinction.'

To hear this, one would think that Charles had always spoken straight from the heart. That was far from the truth. He carried on a daily battle, with its victories and defeats, a struggle that lasted to the end of his life. The 'hermit' and the 'universal brother' were always at war within him.

By nature, Charles loved solitude and order. He also thought that they were indispensable for a monk: 'My vocation is enclosure'. He decided to build a 'cloister wall which will entirely surround the site'. He never managed it. 'As soon as I can, I shall surround the whole site with a wire fence to stop people coming in.'

The problem was a very real one. 'Inwardly, I reproach myself for not giving enough time to prayer . . . in the daytime they never stop knocking on my door, and at night (which would be the proper time), I am so wretchedly tired that I just drop off to sleep.' He no longer even heard his alarm ring. 'I do things just by routine, while I am really asleep' . . . 'I attach too much importance to *my* time.' It was hardly surprising that he should experience 'lassitude, distractions, and constant emptiness in prayer'.

He made himself a timetable. But it was a hermit's timetable. He had forgotten to allow even a minute in it for a visitor. How could he be a 'universal brother' if he kept to such a timetable? That was the struggle within.

By instinct Charles tried to give visitors as 'little time as possible'. It was his bishop who advised him to 'arrange benches about the place . . . and make the visitors sit down, instead of leaving them to stand there'. Charles also noted that he remained a certain distance from guests because he was afraid of lice.

And what was he to do when faced with an invasion of a hundred people a day? On one occasion, in desperation he let some visiting soldiers chase away the flood of guests. At other times he bawled out like an officer to put some order into the mêlée. There were days when his nerves just could not take it. Especially when some of his petitioners deceived him.

What was he to do? 'To give to whomsoever asked' would mean, in the 'case of this lazy, impudent band of beggars, doing more harm than good. Moreover, I am afraid that sometimes I am going to turn away some really poor people along with the cheats'.

Eventually he wondered if it would not be better to move the fraternity to a quieter spot. The inward conflict became serious.

Charles thought about it during his retreats. The result was that he noted on fifteen occasions his resolution to 'enter into affectionate relations' with people 'while trying less to give money and more to bestow on them my brotherly tenderness, and my time.' He had reached a turning-point.

Among all the Gospel verses which Charles had noted down, one by a long way holds the record for frequent quotation: 'Everything that you have done to one of these my brothers you have done to me'.

But what about the importunate beggars, and the poor with their lice? Was the divine Partner hidden under their rags? Could the Partner have lice?

16

A monastery as big as the starry sky

January 1904 – January 1905. The Sahara.

The caravan was impressive. Over a hundred camels were strung out along the horizon. Charles had a riding camel and a baggage camel for his things.

Where was the caravan going? To Morocco? No. At this time of day they must be heading due south, into Touareg country.

A small but rather unusual man was responsible for the enterprise. He was a close friend of Charles's – Major Laperrine. What was his dream? To cross the Sahara from north to south, so that the French Peace could prevail there. Without any authorization at all!

Laperrine was an idealist. As far as possible, he was determined not to use powder or shot, and to spill no blood. His weapon was 'fraternization'.

Foucauld seemed to him an ideal trump card to help put his ideas into practice. He was the apostle of Fraternity and of France. He thought of leaving Charles in the Hoggar. 'But,' he added, 'I should prefer them to get used to seeing him without any bayonets around him.'

Laperrine was casting the bait. For three months Charles did not bite. Morocco remained forbidden territory. Patiently, Laperrine threw out the bait once more.

This time Charles bit hard.

Morocco might well be forbidden . . . Not knowing what was to come, Charles decided to go with Laperrine.

The usual stages were twenty-five miles a day, at the slow pace of loaded camels. After two hours walking in the morning, everyone got up on their mounts.

Only Charles went on walking, at a rapid pace, half bent-down to the ground. He led his camel by its reins. That seemed to him more in keeping with the image of Jesus, and he also wanted to look after the camels which his family had paid for. Once, one of the officers had expressly to order him to get up on the beast. Charles chatted pleasantly until the rest-place was reached.

Otherwise he did not say much. He rarely became animated. But he would laugh loudly at Laperrine's splendid stories.

In the evening, when they had reached the stopping place, the officers and Charles would sit cross-legged to eat, and enter into lively discussion. Charles had a healthy appetite.

The journey was far from regular. Sometimes it was real desert and they went faster. Sometimes the red patches of Touareg tents were dotted here and there on the sun-dazzling sand. Then, 'we went from well to well, to the pastures more frequented by the nomads, stopping among them, spending several days there'.

Charles did not visit the tents without some apprehension. For the first time in his Christian life, it was he who made the first step in contacting people. He felt rather shy.

After the usual greetings, he distributed medicine, some alms, mirrors, thread and needles. The ice was broken. He began to study Tamahaq, the language of the Touareg.

He always carried a notebook made of old envelopes. It hung from his belt. In the daytime he took notes, under a Touareg tent, or on the march. Until late at night, by the light of a candle in his military tent, he would rearrange and recopy his notes.

Was the scientist in de Foucauld coming to life again? Laperrine thought so: 'Faced with his life of adventure, the Foucauld of Morocco returned; he missed his sextant'.

Something else reminded Charles of Morocco. During this journey he made a statement to be found nowhere else in his writings: 'Among other graces, I have had one which I have been asking Jesus for for a long time, that is, for love of him, to live as uncomfortably as I lived pleasurably in Morocco'.

He no longer had a fixed roof over his head. He was leading a nomadic life. He depended on others' hospitality. Once again he made the acquaintance of lice . . . super white lice with a black line on their backs.

They crossed the Hoggar (which we have already encountered in the first chapter). They stayed in attractive little villages. 'As soon as I can manage a fixed residence, I shall do so.'

But the caravan was turning north again. 'Not so much out of fear of the Touareg as from fear of certain Frenchmen, Laperrine would not allow me just now to stay in the Hoggar. Later on, perhaps.' After a year's travelling, Charles returned to Beni Abbes.

He was exhausted, both physically and mentally. 'I can stand up, but I have terrible headaches, and fever and a whole bunch of illnesses'. 'I need to rest . . . it is not spiritual solitude which worries me but the lack of material solitude.' He spoke of the 'distractions on the way which are hardly favourable to the spirit of prayer'.

Once the journey was at an end he went into retreat. Strange to say, his notes record, repeated twenty-five times, his decision 'to observe very closely . . . the rule of the Little Brothers'. Until now he had not had a chance to follow it.

Stranger still, he decided to stay at Beni Abbes, unless a chance of leaving for Morocco came up.

What about the Hoggar then? Was it all pointless? At least, he had with him his translation of the four Gospels into Touareg. He had done it in two months!

17
'This abandoned spot'

25 June 1905. Near the well of In Ouzzel.

Here we are again near the Mali frontier, under the merciless sun of a Saharan summer. And there is Musa, son of Amastane, and his Elders, and Foucauld and the military column. (Do you remember Chapter 3?)

But surely Charles intended to stay at Beni Abbes? Indeed he did.

But Laperrine, the little major with the pointed beard, had sent him two letters in quick succession, asking him to return to the Hoggar.

Charles rejected the invitation, 'however seductive it seemed'. 'I had decided to stay at Beni Abbes.' He was sure, or had persuaded himself, that his vocation lay in the monastic life.

Of course that did not prevent him from continually thinking of the Hoggar. The bishop was reticent but eventually telegraphed Charles: 'Incline to think you should accept invitation'. Charles left for the south like a rocket. He had been at Beni Abbes no longer than three and a half months.

Here we are, then, at the well of In Ouzzel. At last we are moving in the direction of the Hoggar.

Only on the way did the marabout's plans take shape. 'I lived for each day alone,' '*Your* life at Nazareth can be lived anywhere . . . so lead it where it is most useful to one's neighbour.'

The establishment itself became clearer: 'I am going to set myself up for a few months, perhaps for longer, in this region, in the village of Tamanrasset . . . I don't think that I should allow this door, once opened, to be closed . . . I am going to set myself up without making any plans'.

Imperceptibly, the altitude was increasing. The sun became less intolerable. Dunes, sand, stones, gorges, valleys and mountains succeeded one another in never-ending line.

Then, suddenly, in the distance, the Hoggar range came into

sight. It was a kind of fairy-tale castle with impregnable towers.

On 11 August, Charles noted: 'I chose Tamanrasset, a village of twenty families in the middle of the mountain, at the heart of the Hoggar and of Dag Rali, its main limb, away from all the major centres. It does not seem possible that there could ever be any garrison, telegraph or European here, and there will not be a mission for a long time. I chose this distant spot where I want the only model for my life to be the life of Jesus of Nazareth'.

This was the essential Charles de Foucauld; Nazareth as a central point and a forgotten corner.

They discovered this point almost 4600 feet up. Surrounded by mountains, it was a plain varying in width between three and six miles.

The column advanced over the white sand of the great plain. Here and there were rare tufts of half-dead grass.

On the edge of the oued there were about twenty reed huts, scattered over more than a kilometre. And a few wells. There were also a few worn-out fields of corn. Only millet and a few tomato plants allowed a touch of greenery at the end of summer. This was the 'hamlet' of the Harratines. They were black-skinned crofters who looked after the wheat and barley of the Touareg.

The day was coming to an end. Something miraculous was happening. While the sand of the wadi grew less pale, the mountains in the north and in the west came to life. Towering over everything, one peak was nearly 10,000 feet high; it glittered far in the distance, to the west of the range.

The mountains seemed to catch fire. They became inflamed from foot to summit as the sun descended. Roseate, red and purple flames succeeded one another. In the distance the range took on a bluish-violet tint. Rapidly the fireworks went out. The sky up above turned a magnificent turquoise blue tinged with pink. The starry night was ready to make its entrance.

In this August of 1905, the fresh night was very welcome after the southern heat. They even needed a coverlet for the night.

The column decided to stay a while. Musa had brought all the important people together. It was he who decided on the precise spot where Charles was to set himself up: three or four hundred yards from the first Harratine huts.

Charles sold his camels. He had to pay for the house to be built, for the well and for a small garden.

'My house consisted of two rooms each 1.75 m. wide and 2.75 m. long (5 ft 9 in. by 9 ft); it was almost 2m. high (6 ft 8 in.) and built of stone and earth.' These are impossible dimensions. The bad ventilation would ensure that anyone in it would suffocate.

'Later they built a reed hut which was the parlour, refectory, and kitchen . . . a place for entertaining.' It makes one smile to read these monastic terms – parlour and refectory. A reed hut! But there at least he would not stifle.

'To make sure that the Blessed Sacrament is safe, I shall sleep near it.'

The work went ahead. The column rested. Charles was photographed in front of his house.

'Tomorrow morning the French detachment will leave here.' It was 3 September. The marabout was 750 miles from Beni Abbes. Sixty days' from the little railway.

In a few days he would be forty-seven years of age.

18
'A very simple family life'

So there was Charles at Tamanrasset. Suddenly a twelve-year-old dream seemed to have vanished. How could he establish in this desolate place anything remotely resembling his 'Little Brothers and Little Sisters'?

Everything had started barely three years after he had entered the monastery, as we have seen. Six months before leaving it, he had prepared his rule. It covered little more than a sheet of business paper. Charles's tiny writing was all over it.

It was about leading the life of Jesus of Nazareth in non-Christian countries. They would live in groups of ten to eighteen brothers. It was full of the breath of the Gospel. It was splendid – but it was unlivable.

We can guess the reaction of the prudent Father Huvelin. But no matter! At Nazareth, Charles wrote a new rule: two hundred typewritten pages. At Beni Abbes he corrected it and recopied it for the 'Little Sisters'. The eucharistic liturgy (which included not only the celebration of the Eucharist but perpetual adoration of the Blessed Sacrament) became one of the three goals of the Order. He envisaged monasteries consisting of twenty to twenty-five brothers.

Several passages of this new rule are not without inspiration. But how could he compose a realistic rule for the community life when he lived alone? And how could he live alone a rule intended for a group of twenty-five people?

The problem was already worrying Charles before he got to Beni Abbes. His plan became somewhat simpler: 'A sort of humble little hermitage, where a few poor monks could live on some fruit and a little barley they grow themselves in . . . penitence and adoration of the Blessed Sacrament, not leaving their cloister, not preaching, but offering hospitality to all comers . . . receiving all human beings as beloved brothers'.

The departure from Beni Abbes marked a new turning-point in Charles's life. Two weeks before arriving in Tamanrasset he decided: 'Do not try to organize the establishment of the Little Brothers'. And a few months later: 'What I am looking for at present is not a group of men who will enter into a fixed framework of life in order to lead strictly a kind of well-defined existence . . . What I am looking for at the moment is a man of good will without any fixed rule'. He had to content himself with one colleague for his apostolate.

Have we reached the core of Charles's ideas? Perhaps not.

At the time when Charles composed his two hundred pages of regulations in Palestine, he sent Huvelin a surprising letter: 'What I dream of in secret . . . is something very simple and with only a few people, rather like those first very simple communities of the early days of the Church . . . a small family, a small *monastic* community, very small, and very simple'.

Was this his true intention? Did the idea frighten him, for at that time every order had to have a minutely detailed rule? And anyway Charles's tendency to want everything organized would surely have stifled it? Who knows?

In any case, this letter to Huvelin ties up with what he had written after his first journey to the Hoggar in 1904: 'Jesus wants me to work to establish this double family . . . by praying, suffering, dying, sanctifying myself, in other words by loving Him'. No more plans! 'Constitutions, rules, are never in the end anything more than useless pieces of paper.'

In 1911, he answered the letter of an interested religious. He went back to the words of his letter to Huvelin. What would a 'fraternity' be? 'None of these minute little external prescriptions . . . but a very simple family life.'

Charles was to die without any brothers or sisters. Did he still think of them? We shall never know.

Like the flowers of the desert, the little fraternities would emerge from the soil only after long years of dryness. A new colour would appear on the multi-coloured palette of the forms of religious life.

From the first rule

'*We want to try to reproduce the hidden life of our Lord.*'

'*We shall live only from the products of our manual labour.*'

'*We shall never keep money from one week to the other.*'

'*We shall be like labourers working for an employer.*'

'*We shall establish ourselves in the towns, but especially in the towns of non-Christian countries.*'

'*Our house will be built in the style of the poorest in that country.*'

'*They will travel like those who belong to the very poorest class.*'

'*We shall go barefoot within the monastery.*'

'*There will be no linen or changes of clothes.*'

'*All our efforts will be directed to manifesting and showing to all the charity, compassion and tenderness of our Divine Master.*'

19
Three and a half friends

Charles had a few very dear friends. The first of them was a Spanish woman of the sixteenth century.

A bright summer sun poured down on a Spanish roadway. The siesta was over. Ten nuns left the shadow of a group of trees. They re-entered their sunbaked wagon. Among them was the Mother Foundress.

Her black veil was worn. It covered an even more worn face. Her habit was of coarse wool, patched all over. She had ordinary espadrilles on her feet. This was Teresa of Avila, founding a new branch of her Order.

She had to act in secret, for she had enemies. The sisters arrived at night. Noiselessly they approached the crumbling house. A few strokes of the broom. A provisional chapel was erected. A priest-friend came to celebrate mass. The tabernacle was installed. The foundation was made in the light of early morning.

Ten times at least, Charles read these accounts of the foundation. When he thought of his future brotherhoods, he had Teresa in mind, but the true secret which joined Charles and Teresa was a secret of love. Both were attracted by the same Partner.

Teresa addressed Him as 'His Majesty'. Charles constantly spoke of the 'glory of God'.

Teresa took the name of Jesus as if it were a new title of nobility. Charles called himself 'Charles of Jesus'.

When Teresa was dying she called out: 'It is time for us to see each other, my Beloved, my Lord'. Charles addressed his 'Beloved Lord'.

Like Charles, Teresa was inspired by the Song of Songs. She dared to say to God: 'Kiss me with a kiss from your mouth'. This was the same verse of the Song of Songs which Charles had copied out.

The second friend was a Spaniard too. But he was now more of a worm than a man. For a year he had been in prison, in a tiny cell.

During the first seven months, he could neither change his clothes nor wash himself. He was beaten three times a week. The blood congealed in his coarse woollen shirt. Parasites multiplied in it. In winter conditions were terrible because he was barefoot. The summer was worse still, for then dysentery reduced him to nothing.

John of the Cross, for that was his name, had committed a 'crime'. He was a monk, and a friend of Teresa's. He had wished to reform his Order. The unreformed brothers did not forgive him. And manners were far from delicate in the sixteenth century.

Did this make him bitter? He wrote: 'At the end of the day, it is in love that one will be examined'. Later still, exhausted and near to death: 'I have no other work than that of love'.

Though he was a friend of Teresa's, their views did not converge exactly. Teresa was active and practical. John did not care for apostolic activity. He was an inspired poet and an intellectual. As a man of prayer, he saw life in its true dimensions. He was consistent.

'If you want to possess Christ, never look for him without the cross'. Charles wrote: 'The more one is nailed to the cross, the more one is nailed to Jesus'.

John had written: 'It was precisely at the time of his greatest desolation that our Saviour wrought our redemption'. Charles paraphrased this text on the very day he died.

Charles and Teresa did not have an easy life with John of the Cross. His views of the cross were not obviously pleasing to anyone. But perhaps it was this austere friend who rightly saved our restless Charles. How often Charles found himself ending a letter thus: 'Pray for my conversion, so that when I die, I shall bear fruit'.

The third friend was a fifth-century preacher. In a church in the Middle East, the brightly-coloured crowd pressed on one another's heels each Sunday. They all stared at a short man standing in front of the choir. He had a lean face, a little, greying beard. You had to strain your ears to hear his weak voice.

His tone changed as he moved from emotional pleas to

coarse, to tender, to realistic phrases, and references to ordinary everyday life.

Social injustice made him explode: 'Reduce God to the level of your slaves. Free Christ from hunger . . . See how afraid you are!' Speaking of the slaves at Beni Abbes, Charles de Foucauld had written: 'It is Jesus who is in this sad condition!'

The low voice continued. This time it was the tone of the contemplative. He made Jesus speak through the mouths of the poor: 'I stretch out my hand in front of your house so that you will feed me. It is out of love for you that I act thus'.

Words of this kind enthralled Charles. John Chrysostom became his favourite author.

What was it that interested John? What he had 'to do'. How to find that out? It was useless to discuss theology. He had to get back to the texts of the one Gospel and put them into practice. That was exactly the way of Charles, who had nothing of the great theologian about him. He was a man of action.

Three and a half friends. What about the half? Alas, we have no room here. Not that it matters much. The secret will be un-veiled in the next chapter. Charles himself was not aware of it.

20

The unknown sister

1914. Tamanrasset.

The mail had just arrived. A small packet which had come from the Nazareth convent.

It was a book. Its title was typical of the era: *The Story of a Soul*. It contained the autobiographical writings of a certain Thérèse of Lisieux. Someone unknown to Charles.

He acknowledged receipt of the book and put it in one of his book boxes. Did he read it? It seems not. What a pity! He would have found the sister after his own heart.

She was a far too sensitive young girl who had grown up in a far too withdrawn family. When far too young, she had entered an enclosed Carmelite convent. Clearly this experience had made her dry and frustrated. In addition she had died too young, when she was only twenty-four, and when Charles was in his Nazareth hut.

With a stroke of imagination, quite devoid of commonsense, the divine Partner seized on this young girl. He used her to prompt the renewal of his old Church. A young person who thought everything was possible entered the arena.

'What things I shall do when I reach heaven!' 'I shall soon go to Saigon [in fact the Lisieux convent did found a daughter-house in Saigon, now Ho-Chi-Minh City].

What? Was she still of sound mind? She was not very well, certainly, for she had only another three months to live. She could hardly breathe. No matter. Her thoughts went out into the world.

These words would have given Charles food for thought. He himself believed that in dying he would bear fruit. Thérèse, for her part, changed the frontiers of apostolic efficacy.

For Thérèse, a universal wind was also blowing. 'A Carmelite's zeal will embrace the whole world.'

'I must enter the entire universe by means of my prayers which must embrace all mankind.'

Thérèse

1. '*I feel that I have the vocation of an apostle.*' [*She was living as an enclosed nun at Lisieux.*]

2. '*I should like to proclaim the Gospel simultaneously in the five parts of the globe.*'

3. '*I should like to be a missionary until the end of time.*'

4. '*I should like to shed my blood for you to the last drop.*'

5. '*It seems to me that there is nothing after this mortal life.*'

6. '*Let us run to the last place.*'

7. '*I understand that the Church had a heart and that this heart was burning with love.*'

8. '*In the heart of the Church, my mother, I shall be love . . . and thus I shall be everything.*'

Charles

1. *'You are meant to proclaim the Gospel from the rooftops.'* [*He was living an all but enclosed life at Nazareth.*]

2. *'I am ready to go to the ends of the world in order to proclaim the Gospel . . .'*

3. *'. . . and to live until the Last Judgment.'*

4. *'To suffer martyrdom in order to love Jesus more fully.'*

5. *'The long distractions, the thoughts which constantly enter my hours of prayer . . . are . . . of the worst possible nature, enough to make me reject them directly with the greatest possible horror.'*

6. *'For me . . . it is a matter of looking always for the least of all places.'*

7. *'Our religion is all charity, all fraternity . . . its emblem is a HEART.'*

8. *'The Gospel will show me that everything is to be enclosed in love.'*

Were these sayings Thérèse's? The second was one of Charles's. We can see that they were animated by the same breath of the same Spirit . . .

How are we to classify such people? Are they contemplatives? Missionaries? 'I feel my vocation as a WARRIOR, as PRIEST, as an APOSTLE . . .' wrote Thérèse. And: 'I shall be all'.

People without labels. Open windows. But the divine Partner is not constrained.

Have you read the two preceding pages? Surely you agree that Charles and Thérèse come from the same mould?

21

The milk of the hungry

23 January 1908. Tamanrasset.

How was he warned? News travels fast in the Sahara. In any case, Musa hastened towards the marabout's house. He arrived at the door, knocked and entered by stepping over the raised threshold.

We can imagine the scene. Charles is there, stretched out on the two boxes which served him as a bed at that time. He was breathing only with difficulty. He did not move.

Musa greeted him. The marabout replied with a discreet movement of his hand. Musa went on:

'What is wrong?'

'What do you mean?'

'What do you need?'

Charles did not have the strength to reply. Musa left. He was worried. The marabout was his guest. Without delay he ordered milk to be brought.

That was not easy at a time of bad drought. 'The goats are as dry as the ground, and the people as dry as the goats.' 'All those who have anything to spare are 200 or 400 miles away, in places where it has rained. Only the poor who have no camels for travelling have to stay here.'

At last someone arrived. Suspended from his shoulder was a small, damp leather bottle. Charles drank the milk. 'For me they sought out all the goats with a little milk within a radius of four kilometres.'

There were other visits. They did not know what to do for him. 'The Touareg were very good to me when I was ill.'

But what was wrong with him? 'Something or other in the chest, or rather in the heart, which made me so breathless that I thought I was dying.' 'I beg Laperrine to send me some condensed milk, a little wine and a few other things in order to help me to get my strength back.'

All that had to come from In Salah. It was not the corner shop! He had to wait two months. Until then the milk intended for the starving children of the poorest Touareg saved him.

Charles had returned exhausted from a long journey at the height of the Saharan summer. At Tamanrasset he followed a ridiculous régime. He hardly ate more than the local people: some barley gruel and dates. More than once he shared it with the children. It was the ideal diet for dying from scurvy.

In addition he was not getting any physical exercise. Eleven hours a day he was bent over his notes on the Touareg language. He did not realize that he was close to suicide. He merely thought that he was getting old: 'I feel increasingly that I'm running down'.

But what really affected him was the daily unsatisfied longing for the post. 'It is three months, more than three months, since I had any letters.' 'I find this too long; so many things can happen.' That was to last six months. It was too much for a man as sensitive as Charles.

But above all, it was his Partner. Yes, his divine Partner seemed to have abandoned him. 'Surely you have forgotten me?'

There had been no Mass for six months. He did not have permission to celebrate the Eucharist alone. [The Mass was a communal celebration and the priest could not celebrate alone. An exception was allowed in January 1908, but it was expressly laid down that he could not keep a tabernacle.] On 25 December 1907 he noted: 'No midnight mass for the first time for twenty-one years'.

Surely the Partner could say something . . . He could embrace him. The joy of that first encounter in Nazareth seemed a long way away.

'Everything which is a pious exercise or prayer leaves much to be desired . . . everything is very dull, sometimes curtailed or too quick, always full of distractions, never satisfying, especially when travelling; sometimes sleep overcomes me; sometimes I put it off from hour to hour and go to sleep without finishing; sometimes I have hardly begun.'

Immobile on his two boxes, Charles often looked at his table where the notes had accumulated. Nothing was getting done.

He felt that death was very close. 'It is almost eighteen years since I entered the monastery. It is the fiftieth year of my life. What a harvest I ought to reap, for myself and for others . . . and instead of that, for me misery, and not the least benefit to others.'

If he had died then, none of his plans would have been complete or even begun. His linguistic labours were hardly started. His approach to the Touareg had achieved almost nothing. His apostolic work, nil. The Little Brothers and Little Sisters, nil. His conversion, nil.

To die alone in a corner of the Sahara, like so many other inhabitants of the Sahara? Was there a mystery hidden behind this death? Did the Partner's style offer a clue?

In any case, Charles noted: 'The means which He used in the crib, at Nazareth and on the cross are: poverty, lowliness, humiliation, abandonment, persecution, suffering, the cross. Those are our weapons. We shall not find any better than Him, and He has not grown old'.

Marabout, you thought you could 'do a little to comfort those poor starving people'. And here you are, dependent on the milk of the poorest starving children of the Touareg. But that was the Partner's way.

22

'Between the horse's shoulder and knee'

Tamanrasset. In the marabout's house.

There was no longer any reason to worry. Charles was better. But what about those piles of notes on the table? What were they exactly?

'I am studying the Touareg language with all my strength.'

In 1905: 'I still have enough for six months'.

In 1908: 'It is much longer than I thought'.

In 1912: 'I need another 15 years'.

In 1914: he made an inventory. 'I have on the stocks:

'1. A concise Touareg-French dictionary.

'2. A Touareg-French dictionary of proper names.

'3. A concise French-Touareg dictionary.

'4. A more complete Touareg-French dictionary. [This was a monster of 2028 pages covered in his minuscule calligraphic writing and dotted with precise little diagrams.]

'5. A collection of Touareg poems and proverbs.

[This was no less than 806 pages in length.]

'6. A collection of Touareg prose texts.

'7. A Touareg grammar.'

How had Charles managed to collect all the material necessary for these undertakings?

First of all, thanks to his three long journeys that he made at the very beginning.

Laperrine had summed him up with his usual precision: 'There is nothing more amusing than to see him lording it, pencil in hand, in the middle of an areopagus of old dowagers sitting on the ground and gossiping, all sipping their tea and smoking their pipes'.

These were women who were well acquainted with Touareg traditions, legends, genealogies and poems.

And what poems there were! All the Touareg wrote poetry, even though not everyone was a poet. They praised God, celebrated love, marauding expeditions, the beauty of women and the beauty of camels.

One woman especially was famous. She was called Dassine. Charles often saw her when she was in the area. For whole days they worked together. The work required much patience on both sides. This perfectionist only let go when he had found that tiny detail which was lacking.

Sometimes he was stuck. A French word escaped him. No telephone. He had to write a letter: 'Do you know the French word for that part of the horse's leg between the shoulder and the knee?' He had to wait weeks for the answer.

There were also visits. Clearly Charles preferred them to be short. 'I am not going to see anyone, unless I am called to see someone who is sick.' 'Old and forgetful (he was fifty-one), I do not want to leave things half-done, because I forget everything if I leave what I'm doing aside for a while.'

In fact Charles worked above all with paid interpreters. He had discovered Musa's secretary: 'He has a wonderful memory, knows all the business and the people of the Hoggar . . . all the old stories.'

But everything had still to be written down for the first time. It was a very monotonous task. When it came to the variant of a piece of verse, he recopied the entire sheet.

But why exactly was Charles engaged in this scientific work? The reason was simple: 'So that I can do some good for these brothers in Jesus'. 'This task is indispensable for my successors and for myself.'

Was it really a useful tool for a future apostolate? Did that work really need the word for the 'part of the horse's leg between the shoulder and the knee'?

It might seem that Charles had only that in mind. He had his misgivings: 'I am anxious to finish in order to give more time to prayer and the people'.

Why did he not abridge it then? Why did he not leave Tamanrasset, from which the drought had driven the great majority of the Touareg?

Anyway, what would he do otherwise? 'Live by making ropes and wooden dishes', as he had planned before he arrived? Work as a tanner and saddler, as he had imagined later? Was that realistic? He had been given the hands of a writer and the head of a scholar. Why not use them? Why be something other than he was? Otherwise the dance would lose its unique style.

As often happens in life, one does some things without much idea of all their implications. No more than a kind of instinct tells you that they have to be done. 'I do not give enough time to prayer . . . however, I think I shall do well to go on as I am, for I want to lose none of the time spent on the Touareg.'

The marabout questioned them incessantly, on the minute aspects of life, on the feelings, even the most intimate, which make the heart beat. He was obstinate enough in the end to find out something of what really made the Touareg tick.

Surely to discover another person exactly as he or she is, is to 'become his brother or her sister'?

To remain French yet to feel with the Touareg, that was surely to be a 'universal brother'.

Perhaps Charles never suspected that.

23
'A chance to revise my will'

November 1913. Tamanrasset.

Everything was quiet. Charles, his spectacles on his nose, was bent over his notes. A few days ago he had returned from a trip to France.

Suddenly the stones were kicked aside by footsteps, those of a boy.

The marabout's ears soon recognized the peace-breaker. It was Abahag's son. Day after day, he tried his luck – looking for some extra gift – a souvenir of France.

The child knocked at the door. This time the marabout feigned dead. The boy went away empty-handed. Charles returned to his notes.

He did not like to be disturbed during the day, for his time was as ordered as in a monastery. He even found it difficult to hide his impatience when he was the object of pointless visits: 'They make me lose time'.

A visit lasted on an average from half an hour to an hour. Of course that was not what they were accustomed to locally, but people got used to it.

Anyway, his instinctive reaction was the same with his closest French friends. He would not hesitate to travel two hundred kilometres to see one of them. But he wrote: 'That is fifteen days lost to the dictionary work!'

What a task that was! 'I wanted to get to the end. The need to work at it without stopping keeps me in the one spot, and stops me going to see people as much as I should like.'

Of course we have to ask if he would have acted differently if he had not had this particular burden. It was difficult to conceive of Charles de Foucauld lounging in a tent, carelessly knocking off flies. He was a workaholic. In Nazareth he had covered two hundred pages in only ten days of retreat. At Beni Abbes, one of his retreat resolutions is truly amazing when one knows the sort of life he led: 'Remove from life all slowness, sloth, and loss of time'.

Such statements as, 'My resolution today is to work with all my strength and increasingly hard on the dictionaries' recur with clockwork regularity.

In this Sahara where watches were unknown, he advised a French doctor: 'Look after your minutes. Time is action'. The doctor noted later: 'I felt . . . that he demanded, if one was to earn his respect, actions and work without respite'.

In 1911, Charles spent five months in a little house which he had had built for him some 9000 feet up on the Assekrem plateau, at the centre of the Ahaggar range. He wanted to be closer to the nomads there. There was almost no one within a radius of twenty miles. Drought had emptied the region.

Would he profit from that in order to enjoy at his ease the unique and indescribable countryside? No question of that! He had come to work on the Touareg language, and to do so twelve hours a day . . . 'I find it enough to do five hundred metres to see the sun go down. I can hardly walk that much at present, unfortunately, since all my energies as far as possible are given to my work.' By 'work' he meant the dictionaries, of course.

At the end of the stay, Charles was ready to descend. Everything had been packed in bags. The camels were late. Perhaps this was the long-awaited opportunity to enjoy the countryside a little? 'I profited from the interlude to revise my will.'

Some letters from Charles to his cousin Marie give the impression of a man-rocket. 'I write to you in some haste.' 'I am off immediately, the guides are waiting for me.' 'I send you a word in haste, as I am just about to mount my camel.' 'I have only a minute, for I am packing.'

The art of savouring the joys of life and losing time certainly was not Charles's forte. His liking for organization had a negative effect on some of his fine ideas. We have seen that in relation to his plans for founding a community.

On the other hand, Charles appreciated solitude and peace.

It was not for nothing that some young soldiers called him, quite friendlily: 'The man who always finds that the trams are too close'.

'I feel no need of company, I am rather afraid of it.' Was he a monk who just could not feel right in the middle of the world? Certainly he loved independence. But it is not as simple as that.

'This grace of solitude is something that I have been sensitive to since I was twenty . . . even when I was not a Christian, I enjoyed being alone with nature, with my books. All the more reason to do so when the invisible world . . . ensures that one is never alone in solitude . . . The soul is not made for noise, but for contemplation . . . yet man is forced into everlasting debates. The little happiness that he finds in noise will suffice to prove how much he veers from his vocation.'

Surely these words seem written for us now . . .

That taste for solitude . . . surely denotes a sensitive heart? A heart with surprises in store for us.

24

The discovery on the mountain

November 1911. Assekrem.

This scene takes place on the mountain where Charles had hurriedly revised his will. He was thirty miles from Tamanrasset.

It was night. Outside, there were freezing gale-force gusts of wind. Inside the hut the weak light of the embers just revealed two veiled men sitting with their feet up to the fire.

'Visitors come from a day, a day and a half, two days away. They spend the end of the day here and rest.' The marabout entertained them in the little house where his interpreter lived, a few paces from his own.

One of the Touareg pulled a smoking, dusty oatcake from the ashes. The cake was cleaned and divided into small fragments. The interpreter added a few spoonfuls of butter and mixed it all together, shaking the pieces in a copper dish. 'In the name of God!' Each stretched out his hand without breaking the conversation.

These visits were a revelation for Foucauld. 'My stay in Assekrem enabled me to make better contact with the Touareg.'

'One or two meals taken together, a day or half a day spent together, enable us to get along together much better than a great number of half-hour or hour-long visits like those made at Tamanrasset.'

During this stay the marabout had also experienced something new that he probably would never know again. He spent twenty-four hours in an encampment.

A nomad and his family were not far away. 'There are no marks of graciousness, delicate attentions and signs of friendship that he has not shown me since then . . . you are worried about my water and wood. He also made sure I had good supplies before my existing stocks were exhausted. Everyone works and is happy in the family.'

'The Dag Rali, my neighbours, are *charming, quite without equal* as far as I am concerned.'

At Nazareth Charles had invented the now famous expression, 'universal brother'. It was fine but unproblematic. He lived on his own.

At Beni Abbes they flocked around him when he was distributing things, but it was not friendship.

At Tamanrasset things were different. Not long after his arrival, he remarked: 'The Touareg . . . are not very anxious to visit me: there is ice to break.' And later: 'They feel the same great contempt for us that the French feel towards cannibals . . . They call us pagans and savages'.

Relations would develop with time. 'People act very differently towards me, of course. Some are distant, whereas others come now and then, asking for a needle, or medicine, or something small. Others are open and trusting, they come often and are friendly'.

In the evening especially the men, and sometimes the women, came to see him. They touched palms lightly, as is the custom among the Touareg, and began with those endless reciprocal greetings. It is difficult to imagine Foucauld prolonging this sort of custom.

They made themselves comfortable in front of the house or in the neighbouring hut provided for guests, unless the marabout was at work inside. But when he was there he was at the centre of the conversation. He joked, laughed and did not miss a rejoinder. He was just as greedy for news and there were always linguistic details that he wanted cleared up.

Charles himself moved about very little. At first it was a matter of principle: 'I have enclosed myself mentally . . . I do not go more than a hundred metres from the house. I make exceptions for the gravely ill'. 'At the start, it was a good thing; it forced me to be reserved and discreet, to wait for people to come to see me, without having to go to annoy people in their own homes'. Later on he would want to make a lot of visits. But there was no longer time.

The visits close to 9000 feet up were always a revelation. When Charles descended to Tamanrasset after five months away, they sensed that he had made strides: 'I had to see all my poor neighbours: they were beginning to be old friends'.

He could not praise the Touareg too highly. 'The most

courageous people in the world, very industrious, very like us: many of them are naturally honest, they are generally good and charitable to one another. Among them there are people of true probity and good faith whom one can trust: grateful and tactful people. Some of them are very intelligent.' On five occasions he compared them to 'our best peasants' and added: 'often with more natural distinction'.

'Yes, I have certainly enjoyed the Touareg. Increasingly I find there are excellent people among them with whom one can establish a real friendship'.

Had Charles reached the end of the road which was to join hearts together? Strange to say, he no longer used the expression 'universal brother'. Perhaps that was more realistic. Was the path of friendship unending?

25

'Something so rare and precious'

April 1913. Tamanrasset.

The feast was under way. Uksem-Son-of-Shikkat was cele-brating his marriage. He was a young friend of the marabout.

Couplets were being recited by one group, then another. Two women beat drums with agile hands. Others clapped in rhythm. Expert displays of camel-riding provoked occasional cries of 'You-you!' from the women. Suddenly a choir intoned:

> *'Thanks be to God.*
> *My daughter will leave me tonight.*
> *Offer fine things to my daughter.*
> *May the clothes which cover her*
> *Be woven of silk.'*

Two weeks later four men left the village. Among them were Uksem and Charles. They were both leaving for a trip to France. The marabout had already asked about the gun he wanted to give Uksem: 'Obviously, I don't want trash'.

The marabout had thought of 'sharing the atmosphere of an affectionate family life, in Christian households'. He was not aware that he was visiting a France apart. He went from château to château by way of châteaux. Among people who apparently had nothing to do. Perhaps it was a mistake but he put all his heart into it.

It must have been interesting to see them both on all fours on the floor, cutting out the sections of a pair of trousers which Uksem was going to sew. Jokingly, Charles said to his nephew: 'Teach him French. When you come to see me in Africa, he will show you how to sit on a riding camel'.

Once he was back in the Hoggar, Charles asked his brother-in-law 'to give Uksem . . . in memory of me, what I possess at Tamanrasset and at Assekrem in the way of clothes . . . material, saddles and accoutrements, food, cooking things, tools, cash, and domestic animals'.

At Tamanrasset everyone awaited the travellers' return. After seven months away, there they were! 'Those who otherwise kept their distance came to see me.'

What a pleasure, above all for the marabout, to see Shikkat and a second Uksem again. These are probably the only Touareg about whom he had written: 'One or two of them are true friends, something which is rare and precious everywhere.'

Shikkat was the father of 'little Uksem'. Without property, but a first-class poet, he had abandoned the nomadic life. He had settled at Tamanrasset, where he oversaw his fields, which were cared for by the Harratines. There was not a day when he or one of his people did not spend a moment in the marabout's house.

This friendship was well-known. So well-known that in his consternation at the sudden murder of the marabout, on 1 December 1916, one of the members of the gang declared: 'Now all that remains to be done is to give the marabout's body to the dogs of his friend Shikkat!'

Uksem-Son-of-Urar was the chieftain of the Dag Rali tribe. He was still a nomad but owned a house at Tamanrasset. 'Between the marabout's house and my father's a path was worn', said the son.

Charles had good reason to love the chieftains. He had interested the nomad in agriculture. He tried his best to persuade him that the development of the tribe depended to a great extent on their abandoning nomadic ways. An unusual concern for the common good united these two men. The marabout, who was so ready to give advice, was not slow to ask advice from him.

It was an unusual friendship when we remember that the chief had attacked the enemy on the 'Day of the Infidels', and that he was chieftain of a tribe decimated in that murderous battle.

And what about Musa-Son-of-Amastane? He could not be put on the same level as the other two friends.

The first contacts had certainly been marked by trust and respect: 'He has received a lot from God inwardly'. Charles even went so far in the end as to call him a 'holy man'. Right up to the end he admired his wisdom and intelligence.

But the relations were inadequate at root. In the best

moments Musa remained one of those for whom Charles saw himself acting as 'adviser' and 'confidant'. A confidant imposed on them by the infidels. And this confidant had his own ideas about the well-being of the Touareg. Naturally inclined to dominate, Charles seemed to forget that he was Musa's guest and that Musa was chief of the tribe . . .

In fact Charles had not forgotten that Musa was the chief. Precisely because that was the case, and because he was intelligent and concerned about the common good, the marabout gave him no peace. 'I am his friend and adviser and often tick him off.'

Musa, for his part, had a character which was no more simple than that of Charles de Foucauld. He had his own interests. He had his own ideas about the future well-being of the Touareg. And surely the marabout Baï was enough for him?

Musa would even avoid Tamanrasset in order to escape Charles's sermonizing.

26
The wasp-stings

1915. Tamanrasset.

The village was no longer recognizable. All the houses were made from flattened mud, and several of them had chimneys. The irrigated fields had been extended. The marabout's house had become a room forty-eight feet long. The place gave an impression of undisturbed prosperity.

But that was only an impression. Drought always drove most of the Touareg far away. Some had been ruined, for their flocks had perished.

In this little world of danger, everyone was opposed to his neighbour. The nobleman was against the lowly, the slave against his master. The French were against the Touareg, and the tiller against the owner of the soil. One tribe was against the other, and the exploited against the exploiter. It was a wasp's nest. How was it possible to be a 'brother to everyone'?

Look at the slaves. Some of them had been freed: they could no longer be fed. They were starving and lived by robbery. In the little area under the marabout they had stolen grain seven times in one year.

For a long time Charles had sympathized with their situation, but not as he had done at Beni Abbes. 'This is extreme mental suffering: extreme brutality, no heart and no affection for anyone, reckless thieves, robbers whenever the chance comes, with brutish manners.'

Because of the World War, the army did not have enough men to back up the police force. Draconian measures were necessary. Charles suggested to the military authorities that there should be 'compulsory labour' – 'work on the roads. Every brigand would have to work for three or four years after leaving prison . . . he would be warned that he would be shot if he tried to escape'.

Charles's aim was clear: 'To prevent the inoffensive thieves of today ending up by joining armed bands and becoming the real brigands of tomorrow'. It was a question of life or death for the village. But would he forget that these slaves were the 'most neglected' of all?

He added happily: 'There need be no fear that there will also be liberated slaves. They probably won't improve much. But their children will improve and their descendants will be like most of the Harratines who, here at least, are trustworthy people'.

The Harratines . . . As Laperrine said, at first Charles did not have much to say for them. After a journey in 1909 he wrote: 'On my arrival I was very well received and, to my surprise, especially by the Harratines.'

In July 1915 there was a 'breakthrough'. 'A few Harratines are beginning to learn a little French. They come almost every evening, of their own volition, to ask me what this or that word means.' In the autumn that year there was another breakthrough. A malaria epidemic was raging. The marabout, who otherwise had not been seen in the village more than ten times in the year, went there every day in order to distribute medicines.

To protect the Harratines, in the August of the same year Charles began to build a small fortress. A year later he went there: 'It is much closer to the village, which is an advantage in making contact with the people'. Until then he had lived at the edge of the village.

Relations with some of the Touareg were not so simple. 'In general, with the Touareg what matters is not so much the opinion of the chieftains, whose views and interests are always opposed to the interests and views of the great majority of the people' . . . 'The aristocrats are the bad, undisciplined, section of the populace; they dream only of theft, and try to rule to our disadvantage.'

It was just as difficult with the itinerant Arab marabouts. Charles did not mince his words: 'They are usually the worst people with every kind of fault and vice – they don't know a thing and are very ill-disposed towards us'.

Like all the Ahaggar-Touareg, Charles used the word 'enemies' when he spoke of thieves; but he used the same term for the Touareg who had not submitted to France.

Some French settlers or soldiers did not escape the marabout's censure. 'They precisely are the kind of thieves, bandits and wastrels I have in mind.'

As for the Germans, from the start of the World War, he had seen the fight against them as a true 'crusade against barbarism'. All this was rather odd from the mouth of a marabout. But Charles was no milksop. He was a fierce man.

At Nazareth he could speak devoutly of fraternal love – yet there he had lived alone!

At Tamanrasset he preferred commitment. And that demanded choices, mistakes, emotions. Every message from the many opposed groups affected him. The harm done by oppressors, whether French, Touareg or Arab, infuriated him.

The climate of the Hoggar is not one to soothe the feelings.

And wasps sting . . .

27
Jet-black hair dye

1914–1916. Tamanrasset.

The marabout had been counting the days. Eighteen! That was the time the post took now, since the war had started.

It was the only physical connection with 'a passionately loved family and a few friends', 'from whom it had been the greatest sacrifice of all to have taken leave for ever'. He sent all his nephews and nieces a greeting on their birthdays, name-days and first-communion anniversaries.

An avalanche of thirty-six newspapers brought him news that was forty to sixty days old; there was also a smaller number of letters.

There were some from his cousin Marie who wrote to him about twice a month. There were some from his sister or his brother-in-law who wrote slightly less often. And there were some from Laperrine, from Sahara officers and a few that were unexpected. Altogether he had five hundred correspondents.

When he had read the letters, without delay Charles wrote the addresses on the envelopes. He positioned them vertically on the table as if he were playing an upright game of cards. Then he answered each of them in his neat hand. He began by drawing a heart in the top-left-hand corner of the letter; with his '*Jesus – Caritas*' (Jesus – Love) motto.

One letter he wrote is twenty book pages long. But usually letters of that length were already written before the postman arrived, because he had to hurry: the two Arab soldiers who brought the post departed within two days. As far as possible Charles liked to answer all letters by return.

To his cousin Marie, on the day he died, he wrote: 'Thank you for your letters . . . and for the tin of cocoa. You still spoil your eldest son'. She received the most confidential letters. But he also discussed practical matters: 'The women here . . . have commissioned me to ask you for three patterns: crocheted shoes for a one-year-old, socks for a child of the same age'.

He thanked her for a cheque: 'Your gift enables me to make the necessary purchases, so that here and all around here no one will die from hunger (which is meant literally, not metaphorically)'.

He wrote to one of his nieces: 'Here there are two women who ask me for something to dye black the first grey hairs which they have noticed on their heads. What they want is bottles of *jet-black dye*.' A gentleman's charity, helping women to stay attractive!

Every eighteen days Charles wrote to Laperrine, his 'friend without compare'. Laperrine, who was at the front in Europe, had other worries. Charles asked him to 'send me a line of news, often'. On the table before him he had a photograph of his friend, 'which people see whenever they come here'.

'Musa has written to me, and sends you a thousand greetings and his respects. Uksem . . . and little Uksem . . . also greet you'. 'Have I told you that Aklesi, Anagrobu's brother, his eldest son and the latter's wife have died of fever?'

In the manner of the Touareg he told Laperrine about the state of the land: 'There is complete drought here and in the entire Ahaggar. The pasture at Tarat is wonderful. The Sudanese Adrar is good, the Algerian Adrar is not so good, but it suffices'.

Then came the practical letters. He wrote regularly to In Salah, where purchases were made for him. He wanted medicines, tar for the camels' mange, tinned milk for sick children, thread, needles, wool and cotton, gardening tools, seed for the Harratines . . . or he might intercede for a family to get a tax reduction.

Then there were the recommendations. 'This is the best Harratine of Tamanrasset . . . he is coming to ask your permission to travel to Akabli where he wants to fetch his son . . . Your letter will help this Hartani, who is the most respectable man in the village; he is certainly a good man'.

There were also the boring and difficult letters in which he tried to solve problems. This time it was a money problem. 'The Touareg just have not got through to Guitard [an officer]. They told him about weights in *Kantar* [i.e. fifty kilos], whereas Guitard thought that a Kantar was a "quintal" of a hundred kilograms. Misunderstandings all the way. Guitard made his calculations on the basis of twenty-five instead of thirty-five francs per hundred kilos. When they saw that they were not

going to make themselves understood, they decided to take
what they were given, to take their leave, and to come to me in
order to explain the affair, and to ask me to ask you to give them
what was still owing.'

Sometimes the marabout acted as a post office. An example is
the following letter to an officer: 'I am sending you packets sewn
up in cloth: they were given to me by an unknown native on
behalf of Ahmadu Ould Dahmaan, and they are intended for a
soldier in your company, but I couldn't discover his name'.

And his letters to officers . . . Too late, the post is going!

28

A very short phrase

1905–1916. Tamanrasset.

This scene is set in 1909 in a broad plain of the Ahaggar. Musa is the producer, as it were.

Laperrine and a few officers were on a rise in the valley. With them was Musa's big drummer. At the pre-arranged moment Laperrine ordered him to beat the drum. The regular, muffled sounds carried the signal to attack at the other end of the plain.

Five hundred Hoggar warriors in tribal order assailed the French. They raised their spears. They struck their great shields of antelope hide which hung on their camels' flanks. Right up to the last moment they seemed seriously to be about to pierce the French with their lances. But it was only a display.

Where was the marabout? In his house? No, he was with the French officers.

An important question, this one. What was Charles's attitude to colonialism?

For Foucauld colonialization in itself was not a problem. That is understandable, given the period in which he lived. But, all the same, it is not easy to understand his way of thinking. He could veer from the most practical analysis to pure idealism and sheer dreaming. And he was not an abstract thinker. Charles expressed himself characteristically in action.

He knew what note to strike in order to get what he wanted from a correspondent. But it is difficult to know what exactly he thought himself.

An example: 'What a fine task for France's young cadets, to go to the colonies . . . in order to awaken love for France there and to turn people into Frenchmen.' 'The only way to make them Frenchmen is for them to become Christians.' That makes one sit up and take notice!

But Charles also wrote these words to Bazin, a super-patriotic Christian. He tried to persuade him to write a book which would make the French aware of their duties towards the peoples they had colonized.

He was not so diplomatic with one of his friends: 'I suffer as a Frenchman to see the natives not being ruled as they ought'. 'On the contrary, the moral and spiritually inadequate condition of these peoples is made all the worse by treating them as no more than a means of material acquisition. What the natives learn from the infidel Frenchmen who proclaim the doctrine of "fraternity" is neglect, or ambition, or greed, and from almost everyone, unfortunately, indifference, aversion and harsh behaviour.'

He could also speak openly to Laperrine: 'The Kel Ahaggar's opinion of the Sudanese Tirailleurs (a French regiment stationed in the southern Sahara) has been clear for some time: they are as parasitic on their charges as they are reluctant to attack the enemy'. If only he had written thus to Bazin!

Sometimes it is difficult to know what to think of his opinions. 'Progress is possible only by means of a *French*, a truly French administration, which natives will be permitted to join not only when they have French citizenship and have received a French education, but when they think like Frenchmen!' What then was the point of all his labours on the language of the Touareg?

It is all the more puzzling when we realize that Charles was a kind of prisoner. He was prisoner of the colonial system without knowing it. He had to 'operate' in the system if he was to do his best for the Touareg and for France. Without good relations with the officers it was impossible to prompt them to do something for the common good. Therefore he usually had to hide the true motive for his interventions.

It was only to a very few convinced Christian officers that he could say of the Touareg: 'They are a very interesting race – our brothers in Christ. I can speak to them as a Christian'.

The key phrase is 'our brothers'. There is the secret message from our 'prisoner'. Most officers would have interpreted that as naivety. They saw the Touareg as enemies ready to betray the French.

In 1912 Charles started work on a major 'plan of organization for the Sahara'. The result is a true testament. What did the progress of the inhabitants of the Sahara depend on?

'The officers selected for administration must be well-known. Their character must be respectable and trustworthy. We must know that they act not from personal interest but for the general good. We must know that they commit no injustice, that they fight abuses in spite of resistance, that they tell their superiors the truth about things, even when the truth is unpleasant, that their purpose must be to do real and lasting good . . . and not to shine through deeds which look well but are useless in practice.'

Charles struggled to get his plan accepted. It stayed in the files.

'Our brothers' . . . 'the general good'. Very fine words. We have still to see if Charles put them into practice.

29
'Loving in order to be loved'

1907–1916. Tamanrasset.

Some army doctors were guests of the marabout for a few months. One of them described him. 'Before sundown the Father allowed himself an hour's recreation. He walked up and down in front of his house, speaking in a friendly way of everything. He laid his hand on my shoulder . . . laughed, told me about the Touareg and his memories.'

One night stayed in the mind. 'We celebrated Christmas . . . sitting on folding-stools with our elbows on his little work-table which was illuminated by a small candle stuck on the table, with no candlestick. There were no drinks, neither tea nor coffee'. And here is Charles: 'Father de Foucauld sees himself as a very small child . . . he is serious, he dreams aloud, he forgets that I am there'.

All the officers who visited him were impressed by one fact: 'The favourite topic of his conversations with us was the Touareg. He tried to interest us in the original aspects of their ancient culture.' 'As he remarked, one had to understand them . . . in order not to harm them.' 'They had to be made to feel . . . that we loved them, so that we would be loved by them in return . . . we must be human and always happy. We must always laugh . . . As you see I always laugh and show my bad teeth'. Advice hardly to be found in military regulations!

All of them, each in his own way, noticed Charles's laughter and friendliness, his hundred per cent patriotism, his extraordinary devotion to work and his high demands. Many of them stressed his tolerance and his broad views: 'He understood human beings with all their doubts. He was . . . reserved as far as religion was concerned . . . even in his letters'.

Nevertheless, his 'latitude had limits as far as the clearly dishonest were concerned, people who used their power to oppress the weak, or cowards'. Thus Laperrine. 'Then he would be astonishingly indignant.' In the case of an officer who had been cruel, Charles was forthright: 'He is not a good man; I shall not shake hands with him'.

The marabout also had very precise ideas about the ideal Saharan officer. They are to be found in a letter to an important person: 'X . . . whom I recommend to you strongly, is a serious officer, no nonsense there, with the right attitude to the natives, with the right degree of dignity and kindness which never degenerates into mere pleasanteries and a readiness to be easily deceived'. In another instance he does not mince his words: 'As for Y . . . Saint Léger sent me his memorandum on the Saharan companies; it is full of rubbish'.

Charles wanted the eventual new commander of the Ahaggar to be told 'to look very carefully for a good time before he leaps'.

He did not hesitate to intervene in appointments. A careless officer ran the risk of irritating Musa because he was so impulsive: 'Replace him as quickly as possible by anyone of good sense'.

'As far as the non-commissioned officers in the company are concerned, I must tell you that two of them should never set foot in Ahaggar again: Sergeant X, who is known to all the natives as a thief, and Corporal Y, who allowed one of his men to rape a woman'.

And then the inevitable camel stories: 'There are some very annoying requisitions of camels . . . if a hundred or two hundred camels are requested, they will deliver them without objection at the required time, as long as they are asked for in time . . . But when, after having supplied all the camels asked for, they send small caravans to buy the dates which they need to keep alive, and find the camels simply taken away and requisitioned to make up transport columns, they object strongly, and who would not?'

'Camels are often asked for at too short notice . . . others are requisitioned for reasons which have nothing to do with public interest . . . the estimates are too often too low and arbitrary . . . the camels requisitioned are not treated properly but killed by forced marches . . . without compensation to the proprietor'.

Would intertribal attacks recur? 'The main guilty parties are certain officers.'

'You have to be very gifted and respect the natives very much and venerate the hermit greatly to accept his incursions into administrative and political and even military affairs.' [This from one of his admirers.]

Yet, 'He was worshipped by all the Frenchmen who already knew him, and among the NCOs and artisans, there was even a certain degree of pride at being able to talk to Father de Foucauld . . . as intimately as to one of their old comrades'.

30
The marabout's anger

January 1916. Tamanrasset.

The marabout was once again exploring Touareg poetry. The steps of an approaching camel distracted him. The Touareg halted his camel; the marabout raised his head; he scrutinized the hardly visible eyes between the turban folds. It was Bédé.

'Is Muhammad alive?' asked the marabout.

'Yes'.

'Well, then, go quickly and tell his father'.

The marabout knew enough for the moment. He would learn the details that evening. Just think! This Muhammad was the real brother of young Uksem. 'The eldest brother of little Uksem is very seriously wounded; Uksem fought and is well.'

'In an area five hundred kilometres towards the south-west, a region where our people pasture their camels, Moroccan robbers have been making incursions for three years. They have just . . . attacked our people.'

'Musa, having been warned half a day before the attack, collected together all his men, a hundred of them, and met the enemy towards 3.30 in the afternoon. They fought until nightfall . . . night separated the combattants . . . the Kel Ahaggar had six dead and thirteen wounded . . . the Moroccans fled during the night.'

With the precision of a frontline reporter, Charles took it all down and sent the news to his family or an officer or Laperrine in Europe.

Peace reigned at Tamanrasset itself, for there were no camels there to steal. Everything was ultra-dry. Where were they to pasture the camels if not in the south-west? For the Kel Ahaggar it was a matter of life and death.

The impulsive marabout's anger was understandable. 'I hope that X and his group took to the camels, as soon as they heard the news; since he is facing an unarmed opponent, he will

find nothing easier than the complete decimation of the party'
. . . 'They should pursue all the bands they see and destroy
them to the last man . . . Only when all these robbers are killed,
just as pirates were hanged from the yard-arm, will there be
peace.' No mention of prisoners.

Charles was all the angrier because almost a year before he
had written that a 'small fortress is needed in this region . . . If
there is no officer to order it to be constructed, the NCOs and
soldiers of his garrison will become insupportable tyrants'.

But there was a limit. A certain Salem, leader of a band from
another tribe, killed a Kel Ahaggar. He fled. Charles wrote to
the authorities: 'That is shocking. An order must be given not to
take him prisoner but simply to kill him'.

The same reaction was evident in the case of an influential
Kel Ahaggar and his friend. They were both implacable
enemies of the infidels. 'They must be expelled permanently
from French territory, with an order to have them shot without
any kind of trial should they return.' Later, he made a slight
revision: 'To kill them would be somewhat repellent. Perpetual
exile under pain of death will suffice.'

And, still worse: two Harratines from Tamanrasset wished to
go over to the 'enemy' – to the Senoussi, who were at war with
the 'infidels'. They let themselves be taken prisoner. The officer
had them shot. 'This punishment, unanimously approved by
the natives, had an excellent effect' – so Foucauld wrote to the
officer. He also wrote: 'I entirely agree with you about the
absolute necessity of severe punishment for crimes committed,
desertions, dissidence, going over to the enemy . . . about the
need to forbid our subjects from having any relations with the
enemy, those who have not made their submission to us,
dissidents, etc . . .'

One might be inclined to agree that a harsh punishment was
fitting in the case of robbery pure and simple, for in the Sahara a
man without a camel is a dead man.

But these sentences of exile and death for political opinions or
crimes, sentences approved or even recommended by Charles,
are hard to take. Even if he was thinking of the welfare of the Kel
Ahaggar. Were they errors of judgment? Yes, dancing is not
always a smooth business. And even in childhood Charles had
been subject to sudden fits of anger.

It is typical of him that these slips really began with the First
World War. He probably thought that the Hoggar were on the

edge of a blood-bath. These violent or harsh letters were written hastily and under strong emotion. They were not composed coolly and deliberately.

They should not be taken too seriously.

31
The tragic mistake

10 April 1913. On the Libyan frontier.

A hundred Senoussi were proceeding in the direction of Esseyen on the Libyan border. Where were they going? To attack a band of fifty Muslims under the command of three Frenchmen.

The Senoussi came from various tribes. They were a politico-religious brotherhood. They came from Libya and tried to extend their dominance and that of the Islamic order over the whole Sahara. It would not be inappropriate to compare them with one of the Catholic orders of mediaeval knights.

The French had reached the region of Esseyen. In the dunes where dwarf tamarisks were growing they tried to improvise some kind of defence.

The Senoussi spread out behind the dunes. The strategy succeeded; they hemmed the French in. At about 3pm the guns began to sound, and dead and wounded from the French side were soon lying on the white sand. The insurgents called to the encircled men: 'Leave the infidels, Muslims, come over to us!'

The Senoussi were fighting for their faith.

Hundreds of kilometres west of Tamanrasset we have already met the Moroccan robbers who threatened the Kel Ahaggar. They were not Senoussi. Among them was a sub-chieftain whom Foucauld could not abide – the marabout Abidine. He had been raised in his father's brotherhood and was not the bandit of Charles's imagination. He had made the pilgrimage to Mecca twice. He was a fervent defender of his faith.

He wanted no mercy for the infidels, and none for the Kel Ahaggar who were on their side. He had broken with his cousin, the diplomatic Baï. Abidine's ideal was to die with one's weapons in one's hand fighting against the enemies of God and of the Muslim community. He was to lose six sons in battle.

How did Charles view Islam? Had not 'the sight of these

people living in the perpetual presence of God' prompted his own conversion to Christianity?

He had discovered, however, that not everything here was so rosy, just as in our 'so-called civilized nations, where there are also people who do not acknowledge fundamental truths and who are as violent as the Touareg'.

The scholar Foucauld had had an opportunity in Hoggar to discover what the faithful were like. 'All Muslims whom I have come to know are pious.' He translated poems. Some of them were expressions of an especially pure form of Islam. Some poets known to him by name had made the pilgrimage to Mecca. 'Some of these families are . . . as good as is possible outside Christianity.'

But he did not seem to want to know anything about Islam. The finger of his divine Partner had touched him and everything that was not illuminated by that encounter had been put into the shade. For Abidine as for Charles, most probably.

He wrote after his conversion: 'I saw clearly that Islam had no divine basis'. The Muslims? Charles saw them above all as 'barbarians and slaves of error . . .' The most intelligent minds in Europe thought likewise at that time.

Shortly before his return to Africa, however, he wrote: 'All these exemplary Muslims are more virtuous than the Christians whom they fought . . . but is it surprising that the Muslims have erroneous ideas of our religion, when almost all of us have such odd ideas of their faith.'

What had happened? As a monk in Syria he had seen how the Muslims had decimated the Armenian Christians. In Beni Abbes he had thought that Islam allowed slavery. Their religion 'ordered them to kill, whereas ours orders us to love'.

But in Hoggar the marabout had come down on the side of the Kel Ahaggar. Now they were being attacked by the alien Senoussi and by Abidine's bands. The Kel Ahaggar and the French were dying. The marabout knew them all personally.

He was impulsive enough to confuse Islam with murder and slavery. The combination of emotion, nationalism and faith prevented him from seeing behind the apparent manifestations of banditry an Islam which was trying legitimately to defend itself and a patriotism as great as his own.

The marabout wished to protect 'his children' against the Senoussi, Abidine, and a few unscrupulous marabouts. He did all he could to prevent such marabouts coming to the Hoggar.

He had no wish to see these 'so-called Christians . . . parading an evil example' settling in the area.

If only Charles and Abidine could have seen one another with the eyes of the heart (as an Arab proverb puts it).

32
An extraordinary silence

1905–1916. Tamanrasset.

How were her five children still alive? The Touareg mother knew very well why. This was 1907, the year of starvation. The marabout had made his distribution and the children had survived.

But, 'how dreadful it is to think that so good-hearted a man should enter hell after dying, because he is not a Muslim!' Every day, together with a few other women, she prayed for the marabout's conversion to Islam.

The same question worried the marabout. He had been taught: 'Outside the Church no salvation!' But at that time the bounds of the Church were in everyone's mind those of an institution. Hence the enthusiasm of missionaries for a speedy baptism . . . at least the baptized would go to heaven!

This idea is to be found in Charles's letters. It is the same notion as expressed by the good Touareg woman. Each side treated the other as pagan. There had to be something wrong somewhere.

The Koran says: God 'will test you with what he has given you'. 'Exceed one another in good deeds. You will all return to God' (Koran 5:48). Surely there is a similarity between this and the biblical story of the talents.

Charles seems to have understood this. His attitude was surprising for the times. A Protestant doctor reported the following conversation with the marabout: 'I am not here to convert the Touarag at one go, but to try to understand them . . . I am sure that the good God will accept into heaven those who are good and virtuous, whether they are Roman Catholics or not. You are Protestant; Teissère is a non-believer; the Touareg are Muslims; I am convinced that God will accept us all . . . I try to improve the Touareg so that they deserve paradise'.

Another officer reported: 'He knows that wanting to convert

people . . . can only help to erect barriers between the men of different religions'.

'To preach Jesus to the Touareg . . . I don't think that Jesus wants that . . . neither from me nor from anyone else . . .'

What then was he after? 'You have to become a trustworthy friend of these people; one to whom they will come when they have doubts or pains; someone in whose sensitivity, understanding and justice you can absolutely trust.' 'My life is a matter of relating as far as possible to my surroundings and doing as much service as possible. If the friendship gets closer, I say a little about God and give each of them as much as he can take . . . the avoidance of sin, the two great commandments of love towards God and love towards one's neighbour . . . the duty of the creature to think of God, and so on . . . I proceed slowly and carefully.'

For a Muslim the following are signs of credibility: 'A good man is the one who for the love of God gives up his possessions; who prays; who gives alms. Those who fulfil their duties are the true believers and the pious' (Koran 2: 177).

One evening when the sun was going down, Musa and a few friends sat in a circle with Charles outside his house. The Muslim hour of prayer was beginning. Musa and two others stood up, but the others continued as they were. Charles looked at them and said sternly: 'And you? Don't you pray?'

That a marabout lived so simply and in so fraternal a fashion, without pomp and mystery and without expecting gifts, must have given the Touareg food for thought.

But what did the marabout really want? 'The close relations of the young Uksem trust me greatly. When will that lead to the thought that, as far as religion is concerned, the safest thing for them is to believe as I do?'

Charles wanted his brothers to experience his own adventure and find understanding and helpful people who would light the way to the divine Partner. He found them in his own family, especially in his cousin Marie.

At that time when the Church was expanding, conversion statistics were the order of the day. Before settling in the Hoggar, Charles himself wrote: 'Our Lord is in a hurry'. How many times must this man who was impatient and keen to see results have wished to proclaim the name of Jesus of Nazareth? Yet for eleven years he did not do so. All he wished to do was to 'improve' the Touareg. Entries in a register no longer interested him. He wanted real conversions.

Was it a mere accident that the Dag Rali became convinced Muslims? Baï and Musa brought about the Islamization of the Dag Rali. Perhaps Charles was their best aid in this. Perhaps he helped them by merely living his faith. 'May God allow these gifted Touareg the grace of loving God and serving him and may their souls praise the Lord.'

Musa's prayer echoes Charles's: 'May we meet him again in paradise!'

33
'The task of our life'

1905–1916. Tamanrasset.

'When the war ends I shall do everything possible finally to establish our congregation . . . and I shall stay in France as long as possible.' Charles wrote this a month before his death in 1916.

A congregation? Staying in France? What was wrong? The idea was as old as it was revolutionary. It came from the same year in which he arrived in Tamanrasset.

An overpowering longing for pastoral work had taken Charles to the Hoggar at that time. His plan for brothers and sisters living the monastic life seemed more or less impossible or out of date. Now it was necessary to involve the whole Church.

He conceived a kind of 'fraternity' which would be open to all believers, 'man or woman, bachelor, spinster or married, clergy or laity, members of a religious order or not'. He prepared a kind of Rule. Most of the stipulations were taken from the Rule for the brothers.

What about the priest in this fraternity? 'There is absolutely no reason why he should be like most priests.' 'That is the work for all, whether clergy or laity'. And that at a time when priests were placed on a pedestal. 'Priscilla and Aquila are certainly needed at the priest's side.'

Priscilla and Aquila were a married couple, artisans in Greece. Aquila, the husband, and Paul, the apostle, made tents together. A small Christian community with a bishop as a member. Together, they worked and prayed. Together they practised hospitality and bore witness to the Risen Christ. Among the mass of non-believers, this tiny grass-roots community would be the starting-point for the Christian community in Corinth.

Priscilla and Aquila. These names are often to be found in Charles's letters.

Priscilla and Aquila 'met those whom the priest did not see, and went where he could not go'. 'They must be a living Gospel

. . . The non-Christians must recognize the Gospel from their way of life, without books and words'. 'They have to make the Gospel visible though their lives.' Grass-roots community, secular apostles, the sending of the laity to far-distant countries . . . terms which in Charles's time often had no meaning.

As if this mixture were not explosive enough, Charles added a special point: 'It is one's absolute duty to work for the conversion of non-Christians', of non-Christians in third world. Which does not exclude the importance of realizing that we 'have to be apostles in France just as much as in non-Christian countries'.

Charles disliked the ghetto intensely. He had known what it was like not to be a Christian. He would always show a preference for such people.

On two occasions Charles travelled through France looking for new-style Christians.

What did he offer them? With memories of Beni Abbes, we might suppose the worst. More than at Tamanrasset, he was soon known as the 'monk-missionary'. On three occasions from 1915 onwards, he called himself simply a missionary. What he proposed was a pure gospel action which was feasible for everyone.

These ideas, which are both so old and so new, are no passing fancy in Charles's writings. He returns to them again and again in his Rule, even though that contains also some things which are inappropriate to our generation. He constantly remodelled it until he died.

The following extracts from a letter come from the depths of his heart:

To be an apostle, but how?

With goodness, and kindness,
brotherly affection,
a virtuous example,
with humility and tenderness
which are always impressive and Christian . . .

To some without ever saying to them
anything about God or religion,
being patient as God is patient,
being good as God is good,
being a kind brother and praying . . .

To others speaking of God
as much as they are able to take.

Above all to see a brother in every human being . . .
to see in every human being a son of God,
a person redeemed by the blood of Jesus . . .

We have to get rid of a domineering spirit . . .
What a difference there is between
Jesus' way of acting and talking
and the domineering
attitude of those
who are not Christians,
or who are bad Christians,
and see enemies
whom they have to fight.

34

A verse from the Bible which makes everything easy

1914. Tamanrasset.

Sitting at his table, Charles had in front of him a piece of paper two by three inches in size. It was the timetable which he had set himself in 1911. In 1913 he had read it over again and approved it. He now added the date, 1 May 1914.

It is a surprising timetable. Especially when one thinks of the unending hours of quiet prayer in Nazareth.

Charles allows ten hours for language study, seven and a half hours for sleep and about three-and-three-quarter hours for prayer. Under the heading 'prayer', he puts the daily praying of the psalms, the mass, the rosary, and a few short readings. Only twice is allowance made for a quarter of an hour of silent prayer, and even that is for an examination of conscience, at that time enjoined on all members of religious orders. No time was allowed for silent contemplation of the divine Partner.

At first sight the explanation seems simple. Because of the possibility of sacrilege, Charles did not have permission for a tabernacle at Tamanrasset. For six and a half years he was without one. He never mentioned it.

In July 1914 permission was given. From then on, in the same place where he worked, a mere curtain separated him from the physical presence of his divine Partner.

Did Charles now plan to spend more time in silent prayer before the tabernacle? There is no evidence that he revised his timetable, which is surprising.

At first, these periods of silent prayer in Tamanrasset caused him problems. He said of his language studies: 'Sometimes I take refuge in them in order to escape from the thoughts which overcome me during prayer'. And a year later: 'The long distractions which always affect me during prayer are of the worst possible kind, requiring immediate and firm rejection'.

Charles could not keep still . . . It sounds like a complaint: 'My soul is hungry . . . because it doesn't have enough time for

prayer'. 'My soul obviously needs solitude, prayer and medi-
tation. I only give it half of what it needs.'

The time of retreats made in a place apart had passed. After
1909 there was no sign of any retreat at all. He had even made
one on camel-back . . .

What was happening? 'God wants it to be like that.' 'I
absolutely must finish these language studies.' 'I don't want to
curtail in any way the time devoted to the Touareg.'

Something extraordinary was happening. It had all started
at Nazareth, only a few months after he had moved into the
little hut.

There Charles meditated on the Gospel. He came upon the
verse which was to change his life completely . . . It was Verse
40 of Matthew 25: 'Whatever you did to the least of these my
brethren, you did to me'.

Charles's reaction: 'There is probably no other saying in the
Gospel which can change life as much as this one. It enables us
to see everything in a different light . . . May it change my life
entirely.'

That was still only a desire.

Almost twenty years later, a few months before his death in
1916, Charles was considering the same verse. He was power-
fully affected by it. He reacted almost precisely as in the first
year in Nazareth: 'I believe that there is no saying in the Gospel
which has more strongly transformed my life than "Whatever
you do to the least of these . . . you have done to me".'

This time it was no longer a wish. It had become a fact of his
life.

He added: 'When we think that these words . . . are spoken
by the One who said: "This is my body, this is my blood",
imagine the force which drives us to look for and to love Jesus in
these poor people'.

Superficially, Charles was still a restless person with a vast
number of worries and concerns.

But inwardly his life was now quite simple. Jesus is the poor.

On contemplating his Partner, Charles wrote: 'He was called
Jesus, which means "Redeemer". He wanted his name to stand
for his work.' 'Like his, the task of our lives is also to save and to
serve mankind, and to give our lives for their salvation'. 'For
God, love comes first.'

Surely Charles's reaction is a condemnation of pointless
divisions? The believer and the unbeliever will be judged by the

same rule: 'God gives love the first place'. No one has the monopoly, and the whole world has the means.

But what about the first question? Towards the end of his life, did Charles spend many hours in silent prayer? Did he keep to his timetable? No one knows. But is that question important anyway?

Some utterances, however, are revealing: 'I am happy . . . especially in the infinite happiness of God'. 'For me, everything is summed up in the assurance that God is God.'

35
'Most people's lives'

Blood would soon flow at Tamanrasset. But first we must ask what Charles de Foucauld's vocation really was?

It is impossible to give an exact answer. Charles's Partner had a very individual style.

But one thing was clear from the beginning. Charles recognized the true variations of the dance through his encounters with people.

For instance: Marie and Huvelin, the soldiers in his battalion, then the Muslims in Algeria and Morocco before his conversion. Later it was the mysterious Carpenter who met him in Nazareth. Then Moroccans again, before Laperrine and the Touareg.

These people brought the dreamer back to earth. Each of them contributed a wholly unforeseen rhythm to the dance. Charles himself was often the last to see it coming. More than once he needed time and courage to pick up the beat.

These decisive encounters explain the impression one has of two very different Foucaulds.

There is the Charles of March 1897, with such badly hurt feet, looking for work from the sisters in Nazareth. He wanted time for prayer and a place where he could follow Jesus in poverty and humble service. This was a Foucauld marked by the solitary life, by hours of quiet prayer.

Then there is the Charles of 1916, the key-figure of life in the Sahara. He stood for France and wanted to be the father of the Kel Ahaggar. He took an interest in military affairs and structural reforms; distributed aspirin and hair dye; and settled disputes about camels. Overwhelmed by letters, his attention was on the Sahara and the world. He was an exacting scholar, work-obsessed. He found that he did not spend enough time praying.

But he wanted 'to be able to lead my normal life of prayer and manual labour ... while visiting people in various corners of the region'. He dreamed of 'letting conversations go on longer' and of 'closer contact'.

Which was his vocation? Nazareth or Tamanrasset?

Essentially, that is a silly question. The fragments of a human life are like the movements of a symphony. They form a whole. New discoveries could accumulate; nostalgia for that first extraordinary experience in Nazareth would never leave him. It was more than nostalgia, for its stamp had moulded his life.

That can be seen clearly from the following observation of 1916, the year of his death: 'Everything else being equal, I prefer solitude to society, silence to talk, the hidden life to the public life'.

A clear sign of that first imprint of Nazareth. We can understand how, more than once, Charles seemed to the Hoggar a man divided and dissatisfied. The French and the Touareg seemed to be denying him his Nazareth.

But something new did happen in that last year of his life. Between January and June 1916 Charles began again to write a few spiritual meditations. They were very short. But they reveal again the simple tone of his Nazareth meditations.

Five months before his death, he wrote: 'Jesus came to Nazareth, the place of the hidden life, of ordinary life, of family life, of prayer, work, obscurity, silent virtues, practised with no witnesses other than God, his friends and neighbours'. Nazareth, the place where 'most people lead their lives'. 'We must infinitely respect the least of our brothers . . . let us mingle with them. Let us be one of them to the extent that God wishes . . . and treat them fraternally in order to have the honour and joy of being accepted as one of them.'

This was his testament. It deserves to be read more than once. The 'monk' had chosen the life of ordinary people. At Nazareth he had known the God who was God for all men and women.

It was the life of people who are on the go from their beds to the Underground, from the Underground to the nursery, from the nursery to work, from work to the nursery, from the nursery to the supermarket, from the supermarket to the kitchen, from the kitchen to bed. And the same thing the next day, all over again.

The false image of a plaster saint, of a Charles de Foucauld lost in prayer day and night, disappears.

We see him instead as a man overloaded, worried, sometimes

exhausted, affected by the mesh of choices, commitments and emotions which are part of the life of most human beings.

Perhaps we have forgotten the Partner . . . This dancing Master and master Dancer has always danced in the village square and in crowds of ordinary people. The people he has invited to his banquet are the ordinary people you find in the street. It is the little people he fills with joy.

The carpenter's Son must have known what it was to be overwhelmed by work, troubles and people. Of course he withdrew to the mountain to pray. But he was also so taken up by the demands of the crowd that he did not have time to eat. Was his life all that different to that of the average passenger on the Underground?

Remember, Charles wrote (when he was at Nazareth): 'Who would say that the contemplative life is more perfect than the active life, or *vice versa*, when Jesus led both of them?'

Is that the message of Charles de Foucauld? Was he quite clear about it himself? We shall never know.

36
The hand-written Gospel for Marie

April 1916. Tamanrasset.

The news was like a sentence of death. Djanet had fallen! Djanet was the French stronghold near the Libyan frontier. The map spoke for itself. 'After this success the way is open for the Senoussi.'

'On 7 April, at eleven in the morning, a quarter of an hour before the news broke, Uksem, the chieftain of the Dag Rali, came to see me. On my advice he immediately summoned Musa's representative.' The marabout took up the reins. They set up observation-posts.

Fifty kilometres from Tamanrasset, in the French fortress of Tarhouhaout, the situation was serious. There were only twenty-five men left. Charles had his own ideas about this problem. He hastened to the stronghold and gave directions. 'I think that my advice will be taken . . . I shall do my best to ensure that it is taken . . . I am corresponding daily with the commander of the stronghold . . . if he is attacked, I shall help him out.'

Charles was hardly back, when he started work again on the construction of the small fortress he had been working on for eight months. Then it had been a question of defending the village against possible robbers from the west.

In July 1916 Charles wrote to Laperrine: 'A year ago I decided to begin building on a very small scale, with one workman. I chose the site with Uksem . . . It is a courtyard fourteen metres square. The walls are solid, one metre thick.'

'During building, the neighbouring Touareg advised me to live there . . . Eventually I took their advice.' On 23 June Charles moved there. He continued to build.

On 24 September there was a false alarm. They thought that the Senoussi were very close. 'The locals are behind me and are ready to defend the fortress . . . I am very grateful to these poor people who could have fled to the mountains where there would have been nothing to fear'. The enemy had cannon, which could obliterate the little fortification.

Now Charles developed a new plan. 'We have decided that my hermitage will be the place of refuge for the [neighbouring] garrison . . . to connect with In Salah.' They agreed that when the next alarm was given, the women and children would flee to the mountains. The fortification was no longer intended for refugees but for warriors.

On 15 November 1916 the building was ready.

On 28 November he had finished copying the poems.

There were almost no visits that month.

On 1 December the marabout completed his letters for the post. Usually the Arab soldier who acted as postman would come along in the course of the day. He did not arrive until the next morning. In the meantime two other Arab soldiers came on a visit and walked around the village.

The sun went down. Some forty Touareg under Senoussi command had halted two hundred metres from the fortification.

Their intention seemed fairly obvious. They wanted to take Charles alive. Once he had vanished from the area, the Dag Rali and other Touareg would very probably go over to the Senoussi. In fact the marabout was the only Frenchman whom they trusted since Laperrine's departure. And of course they might get a good ransom . . .

Charles thought the knock at the door was the postman. He opened up. They dragged him outside and tied his arms to his ankles. He remained on his knees with his back to the wall. He said nothing. The robbers entered the little fort.

The two visiting soldiers approached, unaware of what had happened. They were shot. The marabout's fifteen-year-old guard panicked, put his gun to Charles's head, and pulled the trigger. The marabout slumped and died.

The next morning the postman arrived, also unaware of these events. He too was shot.

Four people had died for nothing. At the same moment soldiers were dying in their hundreds on the European battlefields.

The ground in the little fort was covered with piles of sheets of paper. They were to provide the four volumes of the Touareg-French dictionary and the two volumes of verse.

Somewhere was the little book which Charles usually carried

with him. In it he had written: 'My God, forgive my enemies, and bring them salvation'.

His will was found undamaged. 'I want to be buried where I die . . . without a coffin; a simple grave, with no stone, and only a wooden cross.' 'I forbid my body to be transported.'

His will also laid down that 'Marie de Bondy [was] to be given: 1. the small cross which I always wear around my neck; 2. a small handwritten Gospel (the four gospels in my own hand) in a leather-bound book'. It was the same one that he had in Nazareth.

What would the Dag Rali do once their friend had gone? They changed sides, as the Senoussi had predicted.

By way of goodbye

Charles de Foucauld was and remains an attractive person.
Initially French patriotism made him a kind of national hero.
Later, however, he also became the subject of a cult, and a ready-made saint. One can make of him what one will.
It is time to see him as he truly was, as a real human being and not as an image to fit nationalistic or religious prejudices.
He was a mass of contradictions, changeable and unclassifiable.

The self-portrait which Charles provided has nothing extraordinary in it: 'I have learnt nothing more than to pray alone, to be silent, to live with books in as unforced a manner as possible, and furthermore to speak to the poor on equal terms'.
Yet, in fact,
if Charles had had a normal family life,
if he had had a quite different temperament,
if he had always lived the life of a hermit,
if he had not been involved in the world of colonialization,
if Charles had not been Charles,
it would have been easy to turn him into a coffee-table-book saint.
But then he would never have existed.
Surely Charles gives us the chance to find a brother . . .
Yes, of course, his way of life is disturbing: the aristocracy, the Sahara, the Touareg, colonialization, the preconciliar Church.
But,
to learn to love with the gifts one possesses,
and not with those one would like to have,
to be torn between prayer and commitment,
to dream of wonderful projects and to live in a state of intense concern
with everyday affairs,

to have a tender heart which makes one cry or explode with anger.

to want to pray and not to know how to remain peaceful or just awake . . .

Surely all that makes up the portrait of a brother?

The portrait of a brother whom the Carpenter addresses by his own name.

The Carpenter who is open to start with but later chooses discretion and hides himself in the poor.

A Carpenter who dances to the sound of unique music with a beginner.

Surely this divine Partner in the dance is the true Hero of our story?

It is not a question of imitating Charles de Foucauld.

If one did so, then he would no longer be the unique individual whom his divine Partner recognized.

It is a matter of listening for our own names to be called, and of following the music.

Charles had already told us, when he was still in his Nazareth hut: 'He gives me his hand so that we can go through life together, hand in hand'.

Glossary of proper names

Abidine	A marabout (sheikh), Baï's cousin. He fought against the French. Not a Touareg.
Ahaggar	or Hoggar. A stretch of land and mountain range in the central Sahara. Territory belonging to the Kel Ahaggar.
Akbes	A Trappist monastery in northern Syria. Charles de Foucauld spent seven and a half years there.
Assekrem	A plain at an altitude of 8850 feet at the midpoint of the Hoggar range. There de Foucauld built a hut and hoped (in vain) that he would be able to get into contact with the nomads. He lived there no longer than five months, studying the Touareg language.
Baï	A marabout (or sheikh) who lived in Attalia in north-west Mali. He was not a Touareg. He guided Musa's conversion.
Bazin, René	French writer who later wrote the first biography of Charles de Foucauld.
Beni Abbes	An Algerian oasis near the Moroccan border. Charles lived there for about two years.
Dag Rali	One of the Kel Ahaggar tribes, decimated in the battle near Tit. They lived in the mid-Hoggar.
Day of the Infidels	A battle at Tit on 7 May 1902. The Touareg were defeated. Tit is in the western region of the Hoggar range.
Enclosure	A term from the religious life which refers to a life of devotion cut off from the world.
Harratines	Black peasants. They grow wheat and barley for the Touareg, who own the land.
Hoggar	see Ahaggar.
Huvelin	Priest in Paris who advised de Foucauld.
Infidels	The name the Touareg gave to the French and their allies. Meaning: 'pagans'. At the time Christians and de Foucauld himself described non-Christians in the same terms.

In Ouzzel	Place on the border between Algeria and Mali. De Foucauld and Mussa Ag Amastane met there for the first time.
In Salah	700 km to the north of Tamanrasset. An oasis where Charles made purchases.
Kel Ahaggar	One of the Touareg tribes to which several others, such as the Dag Rali, belong.
Kel Ajier	A Touareg tribe living on the Libyan border. Enemies of the Kel Ahaggar.
Lacroix	Director of the Department for Native Affairs and Military Personnel in the colonized Sahara. Obtained permission for Charles to live in the Sahara.
Laperrine	Commander in charge of the oases in the Sahara. Charles's personal friend.
Marabout	Also sheikh. A man of God. Usually the head of a brotherhood. The marabouts were never recognized by Islam proper, but their influence in northern and western Africa was considerable.
Marabout, The	Charles de Foucauld was known to the Touareg and some Frenchmen as 'the marabout'.
Marie de Blic	Charles de Foucauld's sister.
Marie de Bondy	De Foucauld's cousin.
Musa Ag Amastane	Chief of the Kel Ahaggar tribe.
Oued	Saharan river bed – usually dry.
Shikkat	A Dag Rali Touareg. Charles's friend.
Senoussi	Member of the Sanûsiyya, a politico-religious brotherhood organized along military lines. Its base was in Libya (formerly, Tripolitania).
Tabernacle	Sacred box or chest in Catholic churches where the Blessed Sacrament is reserved.
Tamanrasset	Name of the wadi, and also the name of the village.
Touareg	A collective name for all Touareg tribes, which also included the Kel Ahaggar. The singular is [a] 'Targui'.
Uksem Ag Shikkat	The young Uksem who accompanied Charles de Foucauld to France.

| Uksem Ag Urar | Chief of the Dag Rali, one of the Kel Ahaggar tribes. Charles's friend. |
| Wadi | A Saharan river-bed containing water only after rainfall. |

Biographical summary

1858   *15 September*. Born in Strasbourg.

1864   Orphaned from both parents.

1870   Franco-Prussian war. Fled Alsace and settled in Nancy.

1874   *11 April*. Marriage of his cousin Marie.
        October, begins military training.
        End of the year, loss of faith.

1878   *3 February*. Death of grandfather.

1881   *March*. Transferred to reserves for undisciplined behaviour.
        Moves to Evian, Switzerland.
        May, rejoins army.
        Campaign in Algeria.

1882   *January*. Leaves army.
        March 1882 to May 1883, in Algiers preparing journey to Morocco.

1883   *25 June to 23 May 1884*, journey through Morocco.

1886   *February*, moves to Paris.
        29 or 30 October, conversion.

1888   *End November*, begins pilgrimage to Holy Land.

1889   *5 January*, at Nazareth.
        14 January, returns to Paris.

1890   *16 January*, enters Our Lady of the Snows Trappist monastery in France.
        June, transfers to the Trappist monastery at Akbes.

1892   *2 February*, first vows.

1893   *February*, begins theological studies.
        First elements of a Rule.

1896   *June*, first Rule ready.
        September, sent to Rome to study theology.

1897   *23 January*, confirmation of his Nazareth vocation by the Trappist General. Leaves the Order.
        10 March, servant of the Poor Clares in Nazareth.

1898   Preparation of new Rules until 1899.
1900   *16 August*, arrives in France.
        End August, decision to seek ordination.
        29 September, arrives at Our Lady of the Snows. Begins
        preparation for ordination.
1901   *3 March*, Beni Abbes occupied by the French.
        9 June, ordained priest.
        28 October, arrives in Beni Abbes.
1902   *7 May*, 'Day of the Infidels'. Battle at Tit.
1904   *13 January*, starts a long round trip in the Sahara.
        19 January, peace treaty between France and Musa Ag
        Amastane in In Salah.
1905   *24 January*, return to Beni Abbes.
        3 May, starts for the Hoggar.
        11 August to September 1906, first stay in Tamanrasset.
1906   *3 November*, returns to Beni Abbes.
        27 December, leaves for the Hoggar with a certain Brother
        Michael.
1907   *6 March*, Brother Michael quits.
        6 July to 25 December 1908, second stay in Tamanrasset.
1908   *31 January*, permission to celebrate mass alone.
        January to March, severe illness.
        25 December to 28 March 1909, first trip to France.
1909   *11 June to 2 January 1911*, third stay in Tamanrasset.
1911   *2 January to 3 May*, second visit to France.
        7 July to 13 December, on Mount Assekrem.
        15 December, return to Tamanrasset.
1913   *27 April to 27 December*, third visit to France, with Uksem.
        22 November to 1 December 1916, last stay in Tamanrasset.
1914   *December*, severe illness.
1916   *23 June*, transfers to fortress.
        1 December, dies.